A Disciplined Passion

Essays on the Works of

Keith Garebian

ESSENTIAL WRITERS SERIES 59

Canada

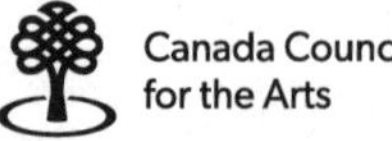

Guernica Editions Inc. acknowledges the support of the Canada Council for the Arts and the Ontario Arts Council. The Ontario Arts Council is an agency of the Government of Ontario. We acknowledge the financial support of the Government of Canada.

A Disciplined Passion

Essays on the Works of Keith Garebian

Edited by
David Bateman and Elana Wolff

GUERNICA EDITIONS

TORONTO • CHICAGO
BUFFALO • LANCASTER (U.K.)
2025

Guernica Founder: Antonio D'Alfonso

David Bateman & Elana Wolff, editors
Michael Mirolla, general editor
Joseph Pivato, series editor
Cover and Interior Design: Rafael Chimicatti
Cover photo of Keith Garebian: Elisabeth Feryn

Guernica Editions Inc.
1241 Marble Rock Rd., Gananoque (ON), Canada K7G 2V4
2250 Military Road, Tonawanda, N.Y. 14150-6000 U.S.A.
www.guernicaeditions.com

Distributors:
Independent Publishers Group (IPG)
600 North Pulaski Road, Chicago IL 60624
University of Toronto Press Distribution (UTP)
5201 Dufferin Street, Toronto (ON), Canada M3H 5T8

First edition.
Printed in Canada.

Legal Deposit—Third Quarter
Library of Congress Catalog Card Number: 2024945795
Library and Archives Canada Cataloguing in Publication
Title: A disciplined passion : essays on the works of Keith Garebian /
edited by David Bateman and Elana Wolff.
Names: Bateman, David, 1956- editor | Wolff, Elana, editor
Series: Essential writers series ; 59.
Description: First edition. | Series statement: Essential writers series ; 59
Identifiers: Canadiana (print) 20240471121 | Canadiana (ebook) 2024047113X |
ISBN 9781771839617 (softcover) | ISBN 9781771839624 (EPUB)
Subjects: LCSH: Garebian, Keith—Criticism and interpretation. | CSH: Authors,
Canadian (English)—20th century—Criticism and interpretation. | CSH: Authors,
Canadian (English)—21st century—Criticism and interpretation. | CSH: Poets,
Canadian (English)—20th century—Criticism and interpretation. | CSH: Poets,
Canadian (English)—21st century—Criticism and interpretation. |
LCGFT: Literary criticism. | LCGFT: Essays.
Classification: LCC PS8563.A645 Z575 2025 | DDC C811/.6—dc23

Contents

Acknowledgements

All of the pieces in *A Disciplined Passion: Essays on the Works of Keith Garebian* were written exclusively for this volume, with the exception of the following six, published online: "*William Hutt: Soldier Actor*" by David Bateman, *batemanreviews.blogspot.com*, March 26, 2019; "*Memory Through a Refracted Postcolonial Gaze: A Review*" by David Bateman, *Arc Poetry Magazine, arcpoetry.ca*, November 9, 2020; "*Finger to Finger: Something Like Intimacy: A Review*" by David Bateman, *Queer Toronto Literary Magazine, qtmag.ca*, November 2022; "*against forgetting: A Review*" by Elana Wolff, *League of Canadian Poets*, poets.ca, January 23, 2020; and "*Interview with Keith Garebian for Open Book, 2020*" by Elana Wolff, open-book.ca, November 6, 2020. *in the bowl of my eye & Finger to Finger: A Review* by John Oughton was first published in print, in *Humber Literary Review*, vol 11, issue 1 (Spring & Summer, 2024). Sincere thanks to the editors and publishers.

Introduction

DAVID BATEMAN

> *"But nothing had prepared us for the heat of so much disciplined passion"*
>
> —Tessa Paucha

Beginning with Tessa Paucha's reminiscences of Keith Garebian's early teaching years in Montreal, this collection ranges from accolades and detailed overviews by a variety of distinguished artists and writers. Garebian has consistently revealed, in his daily practice, as theatre and literary critic, biographer, and poet *"the heat of so much disciplined passion."* The collection stands as a testament to an intense zest and respect for the issues and the artist being addressed—an artist whose work has passionately taken on complex topics ranging from illness, to sexuality, identity, and genocide.

> *"Keith sets an impossibly high standard, and for this I'm grateful"*
>
> —Atom Egoyan

Atom Egoyan reveals a similar passion that operates on a performative level when he speaks of Garebian's ability to allow the reader to empathize and identify with particular life journeys. Egoyan's 1993 film *Calendar* resonates for the poet, and a kind of relay of performative emotion is created between the two artists. *Pain: Journey Around My Parents* (Garebian, 1993) prompts Egoyan to exclaim, with admiration and passion, "*Reading this book again after my own parents' deaths makes me acutely aware of my responsibilities to keep them alive and to continue the journey around them. With his acute powers of observation and beautiful use of language, Keith sets an impossibly high standard, and for this I'm grateful.*"

> *"The offspring of a mixed Armenian/Anglo-Indian couple, Keith must have been a demi-stranger in India"*
>
> —Jirair Tutunjian

Jirair Tutunjian's *Overcoming* "*Gharibness*" details an early journey, through new friendship and shared Armenian backgrounds, the ways in which the poet is motivated and inspired to begin a career investigating his own background and bringing new life and a rich tapestry of experience to the page. Tutunjian's shares his amazement at "*how quickly Keith absorbed Armenian history, ethos, the essence of being Armenian, and how the genocide cut deeply into the Armenian psyche*" and how Garebian's poems "*speak to the heart not only of Armenians but to anyone who appreciates good poetry.*"

> *"... jewel-hard and bright"*
>
> —Joan Heney

The poetic intimacy of friendship treads closely to Tutunjian's admiration for the poet and his artistic and conversational skills, becoming, in Joan Heney's reminiscences, "larger than life." Through the subtly bold, impressionistic images that Garebian sees, and describes in the world around him, Heney shares memories of Keith's early days as a theatre reviewer, moving into a long friendship where shared interests and the ways in which sunsets and blue dresses become, on the page, and in the poet's conversational aesthetic "*a hush of light*" and a blue so pure as to suggest "*something frozen within.*"

"For Keith Garebian, Jarman's work must have been electrifying"
—Felice Picano

Felice Picano, a formative publishing influence (*The Violet Quill,* 1980) and artist, poet, and novelist within the queer North American literary canon, speaks of one of Garebian's collections as a kind of interrogation that creates an electrifying bio-narrative. By examining *Blue: The Derek Jarman Poems,* Picano deftly delineates a sense of the social and cultural environment available to queer artists of various periods, beginning with luminaries such as Allen Ginsberg and Pier Pasolini, and moving into a critique of Garebian's considerable contribution through his poetic work on Jarman.

The significance of Garebian's work on Jarman has come through in a variety of critical responses, marking Picano's take as a welcome addition to the work of an acclaimed poet (Garebian) writing about the work of other acclaimed artists, intersecting with various themes/essays within this anthology. As seen earlier, Atom Egoyan and writer Jirair Tutunjian find empathy and alliance with Garebian's performative strategies, enabling the reader to see a wide sense of profound struggle within specific historical periods.

My review of *Blue* (*XTRA,* Toronto) investigates Jarman with a brief reference to another of Garebian's poetic bio-narratives through the presence of Frida Kahlo, and further illustrates the significance of *Blue* as an important poetic document tracing the presence of Jarman as a queer artist, and the many responses to his art:

*Graced by degrees of subtle citation, Canadian poet Keith Garebian's collection of poems [*Blue*] is at times reminiscent of Allen Ginsberg's call to America at the start of an intense political moment. Ginsberg's first-person plea from Howl resonates in the* *opening pages through direct references to the iconic phrasing from the beat poet's masterpiece. "You saw the best bodies of your generation/ destroyed at bathhouses and tea rooms." The cycle of poems in Blue chronicles the life of the gay filmmaker. The prologue adopts an unsettling, pathologizing tone, quickly becoming a beautiful and evocative tribute to the artist. Alliterative word play coupled with gay male sexual encounters and passages devoted to Jarman's films takes this collection beyond beautiful gestures and into a powerful and highly original consideration of Canadian gay male poetry: "dry-fucking the boy next / to you caused pain to pearl / the back of ferns, peers / to savage the two / of you like rabid dogs, / and the sky to fall."*

Blue *follows Garebian's 2004 work on Frida Kahlo in* Frida: Paint me as a Volcano, *adding a sexualized dimension to the earlier work. This pair of poetic biographies illuminates the lives of two decidedly queer artists from very different aesthetic and political backgrounds.*

> *"Starting with his own insatiable curiosity and acting experience, Garebian dissects and lays bare the intuitive processes that make up an actor's inner life"*
>
> —Jeffrey Round

From *Colours to the Chameleon: Canadian Actors on Shakespeare,* to Garebian's work on topics as diverse as Shakespeare, *My Fair Lady*, and the life of William Hutt, Jeffrey Round begins to reveal the diversity of genre and style that Garebian excels at: reflecting the thorough research evident in earlier essays such as Jirair Tutunjian's immediate amazement at how quickly and well researched Keith's works become—whether they be biography, theatre reviews, musical theatre history, or poetry—when his creative imagination is engaged by a new topic that he feels passionate about.

Round summarizes, with a detailed finesse, Garebian's research into a variety of topics and personalities with entertaining details from the texts—ranging from the memories of Canadian actors such as Tom McCamus and Chick Reid as they share anecdotes regarding learning to love Shakespeare and gender role reversal, to Round's resistance to what he describes as "*Garebian's fierce defense of Canadian Shakespeare performance*" as something that "*easily counters our self-negating stance. It is in equal parts refreshing and galvanizing, as he confronts our collective insecurities and takes us on a revelatory journey into the hearts and minds of eleven great Canadian actors.*"

> "*... a relentless and powerful book, with eruptions of horror springing out of the simplest of images ... This personal sensitivity and awareness is, of course, shared by many poets and is not unique to Keith Garebian, although very few indeed succeed in taking it to such an intense and finely etched level*"
>
> —Rose and David Scollard

As the original founders/publishers of Frontenac House Rose and David Scollard offer both a personal appreciation as well as a concise description of how they became engaged by Garebian's powerful words, specifically in the collection *Children of Ararat*:

> "*As we prepared the manuscript it was manifest that Keith was someone who carried the burden of history constantly with him.*"

Coupled with this strong sense of a single poet's poetic attributes, and the difficult task involved in selecting manuscripts annually, they specify other collections by Garebian that they've lauded over the years (i.e.: *Finger to Finger* and *in the bowl of my eye).*

Rose and David also generously share details of their careers as publishers who were able to bring together many styles of poetry onto the Canadian literary scene within their signature Quartet series that continues to thrive under the guidance of Micheline Maylor, Neil Petrunia, Skylar Kay, among others.

> *"... a transformative writer who reveals other worlds and histories with the attentive language and cadence of a true poet"*
> —Micheline Maylor

Keith's editor for a number of his Frontenac House publications, Micheline Maylor echoes Atom Egoyan's praise as she speaks of the poetry of witness. Specific references to the collection *against forgetting.* She gestures toward the empathy and performative value of Garebian's poetic strategies by referring to the poet as someone possessing the courage to look at "*the ugliness of history and humanity in order to explore the humanity of one man doing his best to make sense of his experiences. And we, as readers, can benefit from this inventory of history, family, and expression*."

> *"His own physical struggle with forces beyond his control become his subject and, just as he has done before, Garebian bears witness"*
> —Kevin Irie

Reflective of Micheline Maylor's description of Garebian's poetry as being "that of witness," Kevin Irie speaks of the impressive ways in which Keith takes on a personal struggle and turns it into a poignant meditation—evoking empathy through the voice and the very serious issue at hand. Once again, we see the body of work reaching out to a readership that may find uncommon comfort within conflict:

"Line by line, one notices how such links are made seamlessly, yet surely artfully, as a testament to Garebian's skills as a poet and an intellectual; how easily he can draw these references into his poems as natural spontaneous thoughts, not laboured connections."

> *"...feelings of gratitude for Keith Garebian's ongoing, many-faceted writings about a father he found difficult in life yet worthy of a son's most compassionate understanding"*
>
> —Brian Bartlett

Brian Bartlett contributes a thorough reading, in six parts, on Garebian's repeated father themes, early on inserting a differing tone regarding his own perceptions of his father. This makes Bartlett's essay a contrasting framework that provides counterpoint to Garebian's conflicted relationship to a parent that Bartlett strongly feels Garebian foregoes judgement upon—placing him within an ultimately sympathetic framework by rooting his *"father in an imagined place, / loved without judgement. / I give his ghost ascendancy. He will not be erased."*

Once again, the performative energy of Garebian's work allows differing experience to find a moving commonality within both the personal and the political, bringing them together as crucial recognition of their intrinsically bound parts:

"Despite all the struggles between the two men, some of the most emotional moments in Garebian's father-son writings see them not as utterly alien from each other but as joined through shared needs, especially those to remember the past."

> *"... the father's unspeakable witness"*
> —George Elliott Clarke

We see another example of the father themes resonating with other writers. The paternally inclined motif may act as an iconic, over-arching form of metonymy as the work consistently attests to a strong sense of memory—where the paternal must always enter, even as absence. There is always authority through masculine identity in Garebian's work, and as Brian Bartlett suggested, in the essay preceding Clarke's contribution—we may "*see them [father and son] not as utterly alien from each other but as joined through shared needs, especially those to remember the past.*"

When Clarke speaks of Keith's various themes—among them "*Art, homosexuality lived among heterosexual opprobrium, and genealogy-as-destiny,*" he points to one collection as his favourite. Including the crucial information that *Children of Ararat* (2010) is dedicated to Adam Garebian, Clarke sees the work as "painfully, poignantly ... the horror that is too often the result of politics and too much the truth of history." The "opprobrium" Clarke refers to arises later in the essay when he suggests that a single stanza from *Blue: The Derek Jarman Poems* likely has the same sexual-psycho import for Garebian as he believes it does (or did) for Jarman: "The landscape of your heart's / blue is austere ..."; "O blue, your body chimes / with admirable longings ..."

> *"... a welcome addition to queering the history"*
> —Robin Breon

Breon shows all of this through engaging historical detail, insight, and reminiscence as he contributes his appreciation for the work Keith has done on a Canadian theatre icon—in

William Hutt: Soldier Actor (Guernica Editions, 2017)—whose private life was conducted during what George Elliott Clarke has aptly framed as a particularly harsh period of "homosexuality *lived among heterosexual opprobrium.*"

in the bowl of my eye: A Review
—John Oughton

Similar to Jeffrey Round's acknowledgement of a diversity of genre in Garebian's writing, poet John Oughton states, at the outset that "Keith Garebian is well known both for his poetry and his literary and drama criticism. Some veteran poets find a modus operandi that includes certain themes or settings and ways to write about them that become a comfortable rut. There may be some wonderful poems in their later work, but their approach is no surprise. Garebian is not that kind of poet."

"The incantatory quality of many of the poems ... serves to enchant"
—Dorothy Sjöholm

As George Elliott Clarke admirably—with a fleeting complexity—suggests at the beginning, and later on in his essay, Keith Garebian "*is a belle-lettrist who comes to poetry only through deadly and difficult histories arising from his dual heritage.*" But there may be more to this terminology than meets the bowl of the eye. Dorothy Sjöholm speaks masterfully of this dual tone in her appreciation of Garebian's attention to language, coupled with his love for poetic imagery—imagery influenced and punctuated by an immense knowledge of form and content. She speaks of Keith as a poet who "*pays close attention to diction and line endings. And he uses sound and sense the way Pope suggested they should be used—as echoes, one of the other. But this book [in the bowl of my eye] offers that primal appeal as well. 'I dream unity,' the poet says. And these poems offer that dream for the reader to explore."*

> *"He weaves the various fragments of life into a whole, which deeply touch us ... how surviving cancer helped him to develop an affirmative vision of life ... Garebian's mind is powerful and dramatic, and his books map out a new perspective on the contemporary theatre scene and Canadian literature"*
>
> —Laurence Hutchman

Laurence Hutchman speaks of Garebian as an unflagging, perennial artist who reinvents himself with each new book. As many of the contributors have shown, the breadth of subject matter and the depth of emotion run consistently throughout the body of work. Altering sexuality, fatherhood, unsuccessful marriages marked later in life by illness and poignant goodbyes, as well as his own admission of the wish to continue to write and "*make love ardently*" into his eighth decade of living where "*he dares to become honest with himself... confronting who he is, and acknowledging that those failures brought awareness into his life.*"

> *"Garebian has given us verse fueled by the erratic pulse of being fully alive"*
>
> —Jim Nason

In his in-depth piece on Garebian's recent collection of poetry, *Three-Way Renegade: $amuel $teward Without Apology* (Frontenac House, 2023), Jim Nason poses the following questions: "*But why do any of us need to know what went on in bed between Samuel Steward and Rock Hudson ('faux hetero, Doris Day's pillow talk dreamy hunk')? What was Garebian's need to pull back the sheets and expose encounters with hundreds of men under the guise of poetry?*"

Nason answers the questions as quickly as he inserts them by referring to the John Ashbery quote that opens *Three-Way Renegade: "Rather than be pure, accept yourself as numerous."*

And numerous and highly informative they are, the ways in which Nason examines and celebrates Garebian's biographical boldness—ranging from erotic quoted references to the poems, and noting insightfully that "*Garebian does not linger in last stanzas or definitive answers to questions about this book ... He refuses to be sentimental or moralistic ... By refusing to sleep in the great dullness of normal, Garebian has given us verse fueled by the erratic pulse of being fully alive.*"

Elana Wolff

Elana Wolff's finely crafted contribution to the anthology, drawing immense personal and professional detail, through an intricate and attuned interview format, allows Garebian to speak eloquently of his life as an artist:

Interview with Keith Garebian for Open Book, 2020

"... Speaking of my own unfinished or future work, I want to be read, heard, understood, intelligently interpreted—all very ordinary expectations of a writer. My greatest responsibility is to myself or the truth of myself and an accurate representation of the worlds that made me. Another responsibility, and a very large one, is to the craft of writing. Chaucer correctly maintained, 'the lyf so short, the craft so long to lerne.' Let my readers decide on where I have succeeded or failed—but only after they have read me carefully."

Keith as Teacher
Disciplined Passion

TESSA PAUCHA

Nothing in my education to that day in 1969 had prepared me for my first English class with Keith Garebian. We'd shuffled in to our high school classroom, unruly teenage bravado masking our eager curiosity, and lounged about waiting to meet the new teacher.

Ours was a Catholic high school in Montréal, Québec, which had, until the previous year, segregated boys and girls into adjacent wings of the rambling building. In our lower high school grades we girls had gathered at the sealed doors separating us, and giggled at the idea that the boys might be on the other side doing the same. Which, apparently, they had been.

Two years past the Great Mingling, the added excitement of daily attraction had still not worn off.

In former years many of our teachers had been nuns, and, on the boys' side, priests, but the same progression which had opened the seal on those doors had been quietly ushering in lay, if devoutly Catholic, teachers. By the time Mr. Garebian arrived, lay teachers outnumbered those who had taken vows of celibacy, and even the devotion requirement had lessened. Finally seeing evidence of desire, affection, and even flirtation in some of the adults, the students no longer felt themselves to be cesspools of rampaging hormones needing to be burned clean of impurity in the fires of Catholic abstention.

But nothing had prepared us for the heat of so much disciplined passion.

In walked a short, barrel-chested man dressed in a dark three-piece suit. His arms were a shade long, his black hair a touch slick, his brown eyes a little fiercely dark. His walk was purposeful and energetic, his fingers long and expressive. His voice was pitched low, but most of all, his pronunciation was exact, slightly British, and crisp, and he spoke in fully formed, elegant sentences. His voice alone made us all sit squarely and pay attention.

At a time when strictly top-down pedagogy was edging to the sidelines in the exploration of grassroots collaborative learning, Keith unapologetically delivered a university-level series of lectures on literary theory to our advanced English class over the course of the year. Indeed, he turned my first year of university English, and a good part of first year Classics into review courses.

His standards were outrageous. Like many of us in the "advanced" category, I was caught off-guard, having been accustomed to good marks without much effort, and I found myself in a concentrated competition with myself to improve the grades he gave me over the course of the year. Yet his annotations on my writing were so thorough and insightful that I felt seen for the first time. More than fifty years later I can clearly remember heading to the library to find out about these Alain Resnais and Alain Robbe-Grillet people when he compared the opening of my creative piece to that of the film *Last Year at Marienbad*. Because, yes, his knowledge was far-ranging across all the arts—film, literature, drama—and from the classics of every genre to the new and controversial.

He made us experiment with writing forms—poems of all styles, essays, journalism, creative pieces and nonfiction. We read Shakespeare aloud in class, Keith keeping us focused and steady, raising our standards for our own performances by reading along with us, usually the lead part. Never mind the compulsory one or two Shakespeare plays of Québec Grade 11 curriculum, we read important speeches from many plays, analyzed and explained them to ourselves, read them again. Even the whip-smart well-read rebel boys looked forward to the days of reading aloud.

He gave us names incessantly, of poems and poets, of literary critics, of authors and actors and plays and films and filmmakers, and we chose how much we wanted to explore of all these references. I made lists. Unlike many people I have met, his references were never given to belittle lack of knowledge; it was all given in a spirit of sharing valuable information, of wanting to enthuse. Corrective teasing took the forms of wit and irony, sometimes sharp but only rarely crossing the border into sarcasm.

Keith rattled our high school's traditional propriety to its foundations when he started a little drama group and chose to present Edward Albee's *The American Dream* and *The Zoo Story*. In *The American Dream* I played the vapid Mrs. Barker, and was supposed to remove my dress on stage and perform in only a full slip but the nuns would not allow it, so after some negotiation on Keith's part, I wore a suit and removed the jacket and skirt instead, leaving me in a black full slip covered by a sleeveless sweater. Even that mild public disrobing caused a small scandal. I marveled that such outrage could be caused by something so straightforward and modest, while the dark social satire at the play's heart was permitted unquestioned.

With his unbridled sense of irony, he got us a gig doing some matinée performances of both plays at The Douglas Hospital, renowned as a home for people with mental disorders. I imagine he truly relished watching us perform an Absurdist Theatre play to an audience of mentally challenged people in the naturally absurd setting of the institution that was their home and treatment centre. My clothes-shedding scene resulted in raucous hoots and hollers and whistles —but this audience's rowdy and engaged reaction throughout had us sensing that they grasped the subtext better than anyone else for whom we'd performed.

At the recent 50th reunion of our graduating class of 1970, conversations dallied around memories of all our teachers until we came to Mr. Garebian. People remembered him sharply, clearly, some fondly, some ironically, but overwhelmingly with gratitude for the level of learning we had from him. Somewhere buried in the discussion of competing Apollonian and Dionysian currents, in the romping overthrow of meaningless traditions, in the careful attention given to our youthful writing efforts, in the embracing of all that was excellent even if it was difficult, he showed us how, and gave us permission, to put passion at the centre of our lives.

a poem with no title

ATOM EGOYAN

Over twenty years ago, I read *Pain: Journeys Around My Parents*. At the time, both my parents were still alive and many of the journeys that Keith Garebian shared about his parents were still foreign to me. As with any great writing, his words drew me in. Keith is a wonderful poet and the images he creates are indelible. In the book, he was also kind enough to mention his response to my 1993 film *Calendar*: "We can all be part of someone else's story. I see an Atom Egoyan film that is set in Armenia and I find myself a little in the central character, find myself part of his discourse, find myself watching him observing ..."

When Keith wrote those words, he was speaking about me. I play "the central character" in that film, a photographer who makes the journey to Armenia with his young wife. The wife falls in love with their translator and my "central character" watches his life fall apart. Keith was so accurate when he remarked about "the icons of pain, radiant among the chronic confessions and surface textures." Of all the descriptions I've received of my work over the years, those twelve words are among the most succinct and potent. Of course, this would make sense, given Keith's talent and his sensitivity to intelligent and perceptive criticism. It was a great compliment that he would give so much attention to my most modest film, continuing to describe its "emblems of misunderstanding, interrupted sequences, montages of depression." He even wrote a wonderful poem about the film which was included in his book, though he never gave it a title. In this poem, he quotes back one of the lines my lovesick character writes to the woman he loses on the trip to their ancestral motherland: "We're both from here, but being here has made me from somewhere else."

Both my parents have died recently, and as I read Keith book once again after so many years, I feel the pain he describes as he journeys around his parents in a profoundly different way. I'm from somewhere else now, no longer the central person in my parents' lives. I can no longer play the "central character" in two lives that have shed their mortal coil. Or can I? Just as the child we have been will never desert us, to quote from Andrew O'Hagan, then the child writing about his parents as Keith does so evocatively is involved in an act of keeping faith. Keith's parents and his particular relationship to them comes alive with his words. Reading this book again after my own parents' deaths makes me acutely aware of my responsibilities to keep them alive and to continue the journey around them. With his acute powers of observation and beautiful use of language, Keith sets an impossibly high standard, and for this I'm grateful.

Here is his poem with no title:

> To flute song and drum, a pastoral
> beginning on the mountain road,
> an unending flock of sheep, coarse
> tufted, carry us along to a sad story
> about churches and calendars.
> There is an energy in each place
> that goes beyond beauty.
> Nothing is accidental: the sky
> and the church refuse chance.

A cluster of brown turrets asks:
What does it mean when you hear our story?
And stones pocked by centuries are a mute chorus.
Come closer, stranger. Touch
and feel how we are constructed,
well composed, naturally lit, seductive.
It's all a matter of watching,
letting your eye discover the already
without a translator.
These places make him feel a stranger,
remind him he has forgotten
ancestral dreams.
[He is] *from here, but being here has made* [him]
from somewhere else.
What is the best image for what he knows,
and will it be significant rocks and cliffs
and turrets and the people who made that history?
A church and fortress in ruins release his musing:
"All that is meant to protect us is bound to fall
apart, bound to become contrived, useless and absurd.
All that's meant to protect is bound to isolate, and
all that's meant to isolate is bound to hurt."

Overcoming "Gharibness"

JIRAIR TUTUNJIAN

I am a card-carrying member of the Most Venerable Order of Armenian Hunters (MVOAH) free-floating organization. I've been a member for some thirty years. It's an exclusive fraternity/sorority with no more than two dozen members scattered all over the globe. Despite its violent and perhaps racist name, the MVOAH membership comprises of mild-mannered amateur scholars, patriotic bookworms, and busybodies who get a kick out of unearthing the hidden Armenian identity of famous people. We have no secret handshakes, or passwords; nor do we hold conventions in sunny places. We do our hunting in public libraries and increasingly online these days.

While over the years MVOAH's diligent and dedicated members have dug up the Armenian identities of such luminaries as the prolific "French" novelist Henri Troyat (Tarasian), French Theatre of the Absurd dramatist Artur Adamov (Adamian), actress-singer Cher (Sarkissian), tennis great Andre Agassi, chess champion Garry Kasparov, actors Akim Tamiroff and Mike Connors, abstract painter Arshile Gorky, billionaire designer Giorgio Armani, Russia's foreign minister Sergei Lavrov, race car driver Alain Prost, Mother Teresa, spiritual guru George Gurdjieff … and hundreds more, my contribution, after thirty years, has been a meager list of three people: Canada's ace photographer/documentarian Roy Tash (Haig Tashjian), the great "Polish" actor Vladek Sheybal who made his mark as the Russian chess champion in *From Russia With Love*, and Alexander Suvorov, the all-time greatest Russian (tsarist, Soviet, post-Soviet) military commander who never lost a battle.

Of all the 190 or so nations at the United Nations, Canadians would be the most understanding of the MVOAH's proclivity-obsession. After all, we miss no opportunity to tell the world that many so-called American entertainment icons are as Canadian as maple syrup, hockey, and the Mounties. We are ever ready to rattle the names of such Canadian greats as Christopher Plummer, Dan Aykroyd, John Vernon (partly Armenian), Donald Sutherland, Catherine O'Hara, Neil Young, Joni Mitchell, Leonard Cohen, Shania Twain, Celine Dion, Glenn Gould, Glenn Ford, The Guess Who, Yusuf Karsh (Armenian), directors Norman Jewison, Sidney J. Furie, David Cronenberg, and Arthur Hiller. Then there are the Canadian greats of earlier eras: Raymond Burr, Lorne Greene, Yvonne de Carlo, Walter Pidgeon, Rod Cameron, Jack Warner, and director John Huston's father Walter, who was born in Toronto.

I had been going through a fallow hunting period when I saw, some years ago, a book review in *The Globe and Mail* by a Keith Garebian. I knew several Armenians whose name was Gharibian but the Garebian spelling was new to me. In subsequent months, I saw further Garebian reviews. I finally decided to find out who Keith Garebian was and, more importantly, whether he was Armenian.

A friend who freelanced for a CBC book review program told me Garebian was East Indian. I couldn't visualize an East Indian named Garebian. I had been to India several time and couldn't recall any Indian named remotely reminiscent of Garebian. Then my CBC friend said Garebian probably lived in Brampton—my old stomping ground. In the late Sixties, I had been a reporter at the long-buried *Brampton Times & Conservator* of Lord Roy Thomson of Fleet.

I phoned Keith. Introduced myself. I learned that Keith's father (Adam), had fled Armenian Dikranagerd (now Diyarbakir in Turkey) during the 1915 genocide of Armenians by the

Turkish government. Close to 1.5 million Armenians had been killed by the Turkish army and criminals released from jail to support the army in its butchery of Armenian civilians. Dikranagerd, like the rest of historic Armenia, was embalmed into Turkey. Fleeing on foot, five-year-old Adam had made it to Iraq. From there, he had travelled to India. Some years later he had married an Anglo-Indian lady. In addition to Keith (their firstborn), they had two daughters. In 1961 the family immigrated to Montreal.

Keith knew almost nothing about his father's people. During our telephone conversation and later in person and through email, I tried to give him a crash course in the Armenians, their 3,000-year history, the fact that Armenia was the first country (301 AD) to adopt Christianity as state religion, the 1915 Genocide, and how Turkey refuses to this day to acknowledge its horrendous crime.

Several times we had long coffee sessions where Keith asked me a litany of questions about the Armenians. I couldn't answer all of his questions. I decided to introduce him to the people who ran the Toronto Armenian Community Centre. Keith made quick friends with everyone there. He also began to write poems about Armenian issues, concerns, and particularly the genocide. He delivered speeches at the centre and had several well-attended book launches. As his circle of Armenian friends and acquaintances expanded, he became friends with film director Atom Egoyan, actress Arsinée Khanjian, award-winning poet Peter Balakian, and bestselling novelist Chris Bohjalian. His reconnecting to his Armenian roots also opened the door to exploring his relationship with his father. The result was the collection of poems titled *Children of Ararat.*

Then one day in 2013 I heard Keith had been invited on a writer's familiarization trip to Armenia, along with half-a-dozen Armenian writers from around the world. During his visit, he was awarded Armenia's highest literary award: the William Saroyan Medal "for contributing to the dissemination of Armenian culture in the Diaspora." That same year, he also won the Mississauga Arts Award for Writing for a record-breaking third time.

Keith continued to write about Armenians, the genocide, and his once-difficult relationship with his father ... and he kept winning awards for his poems, plus receiving grants from Canada Council and the Ontario Arts Council. His work appeared in hundreds of publications around the world and was translated into Armenian, Bulgarian, Chinese, French, German, Hebrew, and Romanian. He was short-listed several times for several poetry awards.

It has always amazed me how quickly Keith absorbed Armenian history, ethos, the essence of being Armenian, and how the genocide cut deeply into the Armenian psyche. His poems ("Deir ez-Zor," "The Walls of Diyarbakir," "A True Portrait of Talaat Pasha" [Turkey's minister of interior and a member of the Young Turk triumvir who organized and ordered the genocide], "My Father and I Rarely Touched," "A People No One Had Told You About," "A Biography of Deracination," "Komitas," and others speak to the heart not only of Armenians but to anyone who appreciates good poetry.

In a case of idyllic coincidence, Keith's last name embodies his identity and his life's journey. "Garebian" is a simplified version of "Gharibian". "Gharib" is an Arabic word meaning "foreigner/stranger" or "a foreign land," usually meaning the West. The offspring of a mixed Armenian/Anglo-Indian couple, Keith must have been a demi-stranger in India. When he was in his teens, his family moved to Canada—a foreign country which had little in common with India. But through his writing, Keith has overcome his "gharibness" and made Canada his home. There's a school of thought which maintains name is destiny. Keith must have interesting and original thoughts about that.

Larger Than Life

"a hush of light"

JOAN HENEY

It was 1981, the Lennoxville Festival, and he was set to review Sharon Pollock's *One Tiger to a Hill* for *Scene Changes* magazine.

"Have you read any of my reviews?" he asked.

"No," I confessed, with a measure of guilt and embarrassment.

He offered to send me some, and that was the auspicious beginning to a decades-long friendship.

Ironically, the first review I ever got from Keith was not so much about me as Polina in Alex Hausvater's Montreal production of *The Seagull*, but about the *dress* I was wearing in the role. He wrote of a blue which was pure, suggesting something frozen within, and that reminded him of a Kafka quotation about the frozen sea within us that requires an axe to break through.

Seems I wore that dress rather well.

* * *

There's an expression he used once to describe the way light falls on a city at a certain hour. Keith says he doesn't remember, but I have never forgotten.

We were driving back to Toronto from another city. It was late afternoon and I noticed how the sun was resting low over buildings. I asked how he would describe this, and he said, "It's a hush of light."

I have never forgotten. It's absolutely perfect.

Any time I see this light, it is always, and will never be anything but "a hush of light."

* * *

Keith is an excellent dancer, and a tireless one. I can say this with certainty, because at my 80th birthday party (last August), we danced all night in my daughter's backyard to the funky, soulful music of Jen Schaeffer and the Shiners. He pronounced it "the Best Party I've been to all year!"

And from Matthew, one of my sons (who has known Keith forever), comes this view: "He's thoughtful and intelligent, and I have always enjoyed his point of view, even when I disagree. He's never at a loss for words." My daughter Samantha remarks: "He's kind, warm, always present, and I like his smiling brown eyes."

For me, Keith has always been a beautiful man of words and sensibility, who is mentor, friend, teacher, and absolutely the first and best person to consult when there's a new poem afoot.

In one of his *Georgia and Alfred* poems, there are lines that speak to my heart:

> Poems palpable but mute,
> wordless as the flight of birds,
> memorials for the mind
> leaving no meaning
> but being.

* * *

Impossible, I would have said, had anyone suggested I write a poem about Keith. And yet, the impetus came from an unlikely source: a new friend—a forensic psychologist—whom I had sought to impress by introducing her to Keith. After a very amiable conversation over dessert and coffee, during which Keith offered his views on poetry and his own life, I casually inquired (after Keith had left) what she thought of him.

"He's larger than life!" she answered. And, so, my poem ...

Larger Than Life

He comes
larger than life.
Kaleidoscope
of shifting shapes
of mirror images
of poems,
jewel-hard and bright.

An actor upon his stage of words,
a fencer flashing steel.
Makes it look easy
but I think it's not.

They come from the hidden, the dark,
the soft at the core of the heart.
Makes them from life's bitter pills,
its sad ironies.
Makes them with sparks flying.

Come too close
and they burn.

Blue
Poetry as Tribute and Interrogation

FELICE PICANO

The early days of mid-20th Century Gay Liberation required heroes and heroines, and found them easily enough in athletes like Dave Kopay and Billie Jean King, but unsurprisingly also in the arts. In the U.S., Allen Ginsberg put himself forward; in Italy, and eventually all of Europe; poet and then filmmaker Pier Paolo Pasolini did the same, reinterpreting classics of world literature like *The Canterbury Tales, The Decameron,* and *The 1001 Nights,* completely reimagined and filled with gorgeous young people. In the English-speaking world, Derek Jarman took the lead as the unapologetically gay artist.

From the onset, Jarman worked in various media, but it was his films that had the greatest reach and the greatest effect. He insisted upon reinterpreting or (and in several cases) *reclaiming* legendary/historical figures as exemplary homosexuals and also as criteria. Who could doubt the integrity of his artistic intent when he filmed his *Saint Sebastian* in what was clearly later Roman imperial times, and entirely scripted in Latin? His *Queer Edward II* took Christopher Marlowe's tragedy of the 13th century British monarch, and played it out completely but with a "happy ending." The great Barococo painter, Caravaggio, was not only casually "outed" by Jarman, but the director presented the art for his viewers as stills in his film; they are constructed before our eyes as the characters in the painter's life present themselves as models.

For Keith Garebian, Jarman's work must have been electrifying; among the glib literati of New York, it certainly was both thrilling and controversial. But for Keith Garebian, it resulted in what eventually became a book of poetry, released in 2008 as *Blue: The Derek Jarman Poems.* Garebian already had a distinguished career as one of the country's top theatre critics, and the author of books about Canadian actors, as well as about how production histories of Broadway musicals are actually made. Several have become standard texts: *The Making of Gypsy, The Making of My Fair Lady, The Making of West Side Story,* and *The Making of Guys and Dolls.* And that was before he before he published his startling life story in the memoir, *Pain: Journeys Around My Parents.* Books of poems would come later.

One expected that what Garebian would bring to the poetry were the same critical faculties but under some restraint, with dramatics less free to predominate. His next collection of poems, 2011's *Children of Ararat,* poetry about the Armenian Holocaust of 1915, both required dramatization and would be dull without it. But in *Blue: The Jarman Poems,* Garebian hews closer to more standard, and even more sedate poetic models—with a few experimental exceptions.

The book is divided into four sections: the nine introductory poems of the Prologue lead off, and in them someone not familiar with Jarman should become clued in by facts, general outlines of the life, as well the poet's feelings about Jarman's life. Of Jarman's parents, we learn, "Father was a lance that pierced / you, poor virgin, in a zone of purges. / He was tall, dark and tough. / Proud of his gender, a militarist." Jarman's mother "was a swallow, fluttering / in her fragile bones / a bird in the house / filled with your father's will." And later on in that same poem, "A Lover's Discourse," Garebian writes of the finally freed adolescent Jarman, as having "new habits of sex" and new trends/ in your art/ confrontation and innuendo / perversity."

The poem, "So You Are Not Loved" begins "Ancient Rome would have married you / to a glamorous boy, but England/ Cromwell scowling at its heart / mows you down."

That phrase about Cromwell is so accurate and so trenchant.

Garebian titles his second section, "Corpus," and it is all about Jarman's work: the films especially. In "At His Own Risk," the poet writes "You note how uncovering a queer life / diminishes it. Fiction is better: / Cocteau's sailors, Genet's pimps / History rarely loved gay men." As though to confirm that, in a 1991 interview at the British Film Institute, after *Queer: Edward II*'s premiere, Jarman said, Filmed history is always a misrepresentation. The past is the past, as you try to make material out of it, things slip even further away. Costume drama is a delusion based on a collective amnesia, ignorance, and fabrics. Vulgarity like this started with Olivier's *Henry V* and deteriorated ever after.

Later in that same poem, the poet concludes of Jarman, "You always look for an aesthetic exit / will never be caught in a hotel room / like Wilde with the wrong wallpaper."

Jarman's relationship to the subject of the artist Caravaggio is the topic of many of the poems in this second section. Of Caravaggio, Garebian understands, "You both lived badly / Died badly –as well ..." and "Death cannot ease the music of thighs / brushing against one another, nor the rough / street boys in whom he sought /carnal perfection."

In another poem, Garebian understands Jarman's identification with the Italian artist "again and again, an insistence on evil / Self-portraits as Medusa, severed Goliath / madness under a varnish of history."

In the poem, "He Was Modern" we learn that the Vatican set up a list of accepted and forbidden images, which Caravaggio naturally gravitated toward: "The boy with the rose behind /

his ear and slender shoulder bitten / by a lizard hidden in the shadow of fruit." Triply forbidden!

The longer, multi-stanza poem, "Angelic Conversations," presents Garebian philosophizing, "These are the poetic elements / of our culture: the wanderer, the giver / of dreams / the stranger. Things / to be slowly rolled in the mind like beautiful beads of meditation."

While in the third section, the poem, "In Water and To Dream" he asks, "Is blue nothing more / than a desire to mirror you / in chaos and ecstasy? No / more than a beginning desire/ a journey into the unfamiliar?"

In one of the last poems, simply titled "Blue," Garebian almost answers his own question. He writes, "Blue wrapped around you, from sky / To your body's blue frost / Your illness was blue / blue-black with affliction / cells singing catastrophically /and the blue, your life / a no-man's land of blue / flowers in fading light."

The book ends with a fact-filled, four-page prose description of Jarman's life, work and importance. It is a fitting, measured, conclusion to this unusually close identification of two very different artists' minds and poetics.

Colours to the Chameleon

Canadian Actors on Shakespeare Challenging Canada's Faulty Vision of Greatness

JEFFREY ROUND

It should be apparent by now that Keith Garebian is one of Canada's foremost authorities on theatre. He's not just an authority, however. He is someone who loves theatre passionately in all its aspects. *Colours to the Chameleon* comes, then, as a rare gift spotlighting one of the least tangible of those aspects: acting. Ripe with insights that say *this* is how it's done, from some of the country's finest actors, it's almost a crash course in acting Shakespeare.

Garebian is painfully aware that Canada is often looked on as a poor cousin when compared to the celebrated theatrical riches of, say, England or the US. That awareness comes, at least in part, from the fact that he wasn't born here and so can view things from a heightened perspective. Be that as it may, we are not a nation poor in talent, as he points out. Garebian makes clear with scathing acerbity that it is Canada's paucity of love for our own, from both critics and audiences, that is most at fault. We do not praise enough and we do not care enough is what he tells us again and again. He is right.

There is something in the Canadian psyche that embarrasses us when it comes to glorifying our own. We would rather not make a fuss, thank you very much. It's undignified. Besides, this is Canada, so how great can it be? Garebian's fierce defense of Canadian Shakespeare performance easily counters our self-negating stance. It is in equal parts refreshing and galvanizing, as he confronts our collective insecurities and takes us on a revelatory journey into the hearts and minds of eleven great Canadian actors.

Starting with his own insatiable curiosity and acting experience, Garebian dissects and lays bare the intuitive processes that make up an actor's inner life—the intangible qualities that give actors their personal glow and make their characters come to life. Among his subjects is Nancy Palk, an acclaimed Lady Macbeth, who vividly and memorably discusses an actor's ability to get inside a role and "let go", while revealing how she sometimes fights her own urges to direct herself when she doesn't feel a kinship with her director.

Similarly, the renowned "singing actor" Juan Chioran deftly explores the issues surrounding an actor's vocal range and technique. Under Garebian's guidance, he delineates the registers that produce the voice, while addressing the question of musicality in Shakespeare's texts. We listen and we learn, finding ourselves amazed by the sheer technical wizardry that goes on, largely unseen, beneath an actor's skin.

With the celebrated Lucy Peacock, whose way of handling Shakespeare's lines is unforgettable to anyone who has experienced it. Garebian facilitates a candid discussion of Peacock's uncanny ability to make heightened language sound natural. In this revelatory interview, she strips away the outer trappings of technique to get at the magic that lies in the speaking of the words.

All of the interviews are insightful, whether it is Tom McCamus revealing how he had to learn to love Shakespeare or Chick Reid discussing gender reversals in the staging of the plays and what that means about how certain characteristics might play out when roles and temperaments are reversed. Stepping outside the text itself, Garebian addresses the dearth of female directors compared to their male counterparts. In this and many other ways, he reminds us of Shakespeare's continuing relevance some four hundred years after the playwright's death.

In his own impassioned way Garebian makes clear that, however we may dress his plays in modern garb or incorporate technological innovations in their staging, Shakespeare's work is not an artifact but a vital part of contemporary theatre. As he tells us again and again, it still comes down to words delivered by actors. The relevance of the texts cannot be reduced to gimmickry. Nor can they ever be diminished or politicized by various factions to the extent that they deny what he is ultimately about: universality.

Whether you are an actor, director, reader, theatre-goer or other, *Colours to the Chameleon* will reignite your passion for the Bard, both when it comes to what is spoken and what is left unspoken in this most ephemeral of the arts. The insights into Shakespeare's plays and characters—indeed, his world and vision—will prove startling and revelatory to anyone who is a lover of acting, of written drama or even just a student of human nature.

A Metaphysical Flexibility
Keith Garebian on William Hutt

JEFFREY ROUND

Critic Keith Garebian has long had a hand in illumining the life and career of actor William Hutt, beginning with his 1988 biography, *William Hutt: A Theatre Portrait*, from Mosaic Press. This was followed, in 1995, by his curation of an anthology of tributes—the theatrical equivalent of a Festschrift—by Hutt's colleagues: *William Hutt: Masks and Faces*. Once again, the publisher was Mosaic Press. It wasn't until 2017, however, that Garebian produced his expanded biography, *William Hutt: Soldier Actor*, with Guernica Editions. It is this version that likely will prove the definitive biography of the actor.

But why the obsession with Hutt? On a professional level, Garebian's assertion is that, despite having maintained a career anchored in Canada for more than five decades, Hutt was one of the greatest actors of his time, comparable to the likes of Laurence Olivier. Indeed, the consensus of critics and colleagues is that Hutt was too big for his time and place, but nevertheless went on to enlarge the scope of both with his considerable talents.

Garebian eventually befriended Hutt and got to know him. After Hutt's death, in 2007, he was given access to an array of materials, including Hutt's wartime letters, his personal notes (which Garebian calls "ramblings" on art and life), as well as archival records of early performances. It was only then, nearly two decades after his first attempt at a biography, that Garebian felt he would at last be able to manage an "unimpeded investigation" into Hutt's life and career.

One of his authorial aims, admittedly elusive, was to "find a way of making a performance come to life again on the printed page." Another was to write the kind of theatre biography he loved to read, and which would do justice to what he calls Hutt's "metaphysical flexibility." It was this rare quality, he insists, that made Hutt "a man for all seasons."

Soldier Actor is comprehensive, with a dazzling array of photographs and personal documents. Garebian reveals that Hutt was not only possessed of great talent, but was also an individual of notable personal integrity. As a soldier in World War II, he earned a Medal of Honour without firing a single shot. (He was in the medical corps, where his bravery was considered exemplary.) What the war taught him was "the inestimable value of a single human being."

Hutt was actively homosexual at a time when being openly gay was difficult, if not downright dangerous. Once again, Hutt's personal integrity demanded honesty in this as with all else, even when it made his life complicated. Garebian doesn't shy away from revealing details of Hutt's personal life and loves. Nor does he hold back on telling us about Hutt's sometimes tempestuous nature. As he warned Hutt when he took on the first biography, he wasn't writing hagiography but a well-rounded portrait of the man himself. Regardless of whatever failings he may have had, Garebian notes, Hutt was possessed of a "magnanimity" rare in actors.

The main body of the book deals with Hutt's career, from his beginnings as an unschooled actor through to working on the world's most famous stages in North America and England, alongside some of the most acclaimed actors of his time. In the course of his career, he performed "more Shakespeare than Olivier," having acted in nearly all of Shakespeare's plays. The text fairly sparkles with names and anecdotes, though it never descends to celebrity gossip. Rather, it recounts the life and art of a remarkable actor whose career unfolded alongside Canada's nascent theatrical scene.

While Hutt may have been a man for all seasons, he also happened to be there at the right time and place. Among his other notable achievements, he worked the debut season at the Stratford Festival, with many more to follow. Ironically, the young Hutt was said to have giggled on first hearing that Shakespeare was to be presented in smalltown Canada. At the time, Stratford was so small he had to locate it on a map, having "heard rumours that it was in Ontario, but that was all I knew."

His colleagues in the early years of the Festival included Christopher Plummer, Kate Reid, William Shatner, and Tyrone Guthrie, the latter being one of the festival's founding lights. The names are impressive and the list of colleagues grows as Hutt's career flourished and his creative genius expanded with each role he took on. Yet, to his great credit, he remained indelibly Canadian and, famously, never gave up his Canadian accent even while performing Shakespeare. To many, this proved a revelation.

Garebian tells us that Hutt's genius lay in a "rare ability to absorb audiences within his circle of illusion." He paints a picture of how Hutt not only thought as an actor but also how he appeared onstage, minutely examining his ability to mine roles for depth and a fresh approach, whether it lay in claiming for *Hamlet*'s Polonius more respect than is often accorded him or in giving *Long Day's Journey into Night*'s James Tyrone a more sympathetic turn as a man brought down by his all-too human failings. It is at this point, Garebian tells us, that "acting ceases to look like acting."

Hutt the actor and Garebian the chronicler are well matched in their abilities and, over the years, they served each other remarkably well. On hearing that he was writing

Hutt's biography, actor Sigourney Weaver told Garebian he "couldn't have a better subject." She might just as easily have said that William Hutt could not have had a better biographer.

Lerner and Loewe's *My Fair Lady*

JEFFREY ROUND

In an age of seemingly exhaustive biographies and prolific cultural studies, Routledge's Fourth Wall "study series" offers a refreshingly intimate look at some turning points in modern theatrical history.

Keith Garebian's *Lerner and Loewe's* My Fair Lady is a distillation of years of the author's intimate knowledge about this and many other musicals. His love for his subject and his impeccable prose make reading it a delight, as he cleverly dissects the personal and the artistic, showing how one helped form the other, in what was to become the Broadway version of George Bernard Shaw's much-loved tale of an erudite Englishman who teaches a Cockney flower girl to pass as a "lady."

Most revealing are personal insights into how Julie Andrews struggled to broaden the scope of her acting skills, at times under siege from the callow egotism of co-star Rex Harrison, and how in real life Harrison managed to combine the role of well-bred Englishman with that of the sexist alpha-male. (With an eventual count of six wives and two autobiographies to his credit—or discredit—it seems he was well-suited to the part.)

Garebian spotlights the contributions of Moss Hart, the "sexually ambiguous" director who put the show through numerous revisions until it became what has been called "the perfect musical." Brought on board after other directors were considered, Hart ensured that there would be a gay code to the musical's making. Garebian dives directly into this aspect, linking theories of gender and sexuality, while for the most part avoiding academic-sounding dissections.

On the whole, there is far greater emphasis on the show's lyrics than its music, but it serves to underline Garebian's mastery of language. It's here he displays his full understanding of the literary elements involved. The result, a thorough yet easily digested analysis, makes the work relevant to today's audiences, rendering it far more than just a lovely anachronism.

Keith Garebian
An Appreciation

ROSE and DAVID SCOLLARD

Please think of this contribution as a publisher's assessment that is both personal and professional. But first, allow us to take a few steps back to establish a clearer level of perspective.

The two authors of this article have spent much of their careers in various roles in the world of Canadian book publishing: book sales, editing, book design, pre-press production, and management, primarily with established publishers such as Ryerson Press, McClelland and Stewart, and McClelland and Stewart West (a Calgary-based subsidiary of the Toronto office of M & S); and latterly as the founders of Frontenac House, established in 1999 in Calgary for the purpose first of bringing out one specific book, then beyond that to publish new and interesting works of poetry. (The company's name, incidentally, was a sort of homage to McClelland and Stewart: M & S was a branch of the holding company Hollinger House, which was located on Hollinger Road in Toronto; Frontenac House was located on Frontenac Avenue in Calgary.)

Our first poetry books were ready for release in 2001. We decided to publish four titles simultaneously, partly because we found manuscripts by four really interesting authors, but also because the realities of printing production enabled us to bring out four books together for less money than we would have spent for three books printed separately. Looking for a catchy title, we called the collective works "Quartet 2001."

Quartet 2001 was an enjoyable experience on several grounds: the books were excellent, the critical reception was gratifying, the authors' own delight—and their enthusiastic participation in the whole publishing process—was equally pleasurable and, wonder of wonders, the books sold well enough that we actually returned a slight profit (no small achievement in the world of poetry publishing).

For all these reasons we were more than enthusiastic about continuing the concept, which led to Quartet 2002, Quartet 2003, Quartet 2004, and so on, until we found that, almost unexpectedly, a tradition was establishing itself. Poets, both unpublished and established, and not just local but from across Canada and even from Europe, were sending us manuscripts. Quartet books started winning awards, such as the Stephan G. Stephansson Award for Poetry (twice), the Robert Kroetsch Award (twice), the Golden Crown Literary Award from the United States (twice), and the Alberta Education Book Award, as well as innumerable short-listings, both national and international.

Critics and reviewers started to pay attention as well: "Frontenac House's Quartet series is one of the best things happening in Canadian poetry" (*Calgary Herald*); "Alberta is turning out fresh, grade-A poetic voices, thanks to the efforts of Calgary publisher Frontenac House" (*The Globe and Mail*); "Frontenac House has established itself as one of Canada's finest poetry presses" (*This Magazine*); "Calgary's Frontenac House has made an impressive impact as one of Canada's publishers to watch" (*Fast Forward*); and many other comparable appraisals.

Encouraged by this feedback, as the year 2010 approached and with it the anticipated Quartet 2010, we decided instead to mark the tenth anniversary of our program by publishing ten books of poetry, all to be launched simultaneously. Somewhat grandly we christened the series "Dektet 2010."

To do this properly, we decided first to solicit manuscripts as energetically as possible from across Canada, and also that the manuscripts would be selected not by ourselves but by a jury of highly respected Canadian poets working independently from us. We gave considerable thought about who we would like to be the jurors, but after much discussion not just among ourselves but with other writers and publishers, we nominated three: bill bissett, George Elliott Clarke, and Alice Major. We were genuinely elated when all three agreed to participate. And, to ensure the process would be authentically impartial, the judging process was "blind." In other words, every manuscript was given a number by an independent reader—neither we ourselves nor the judges knew the identity of any of the poets.

We were both gratified and overwhelmed by the response: more than 250 manuscripts arrived at Frontenac House. And then we waited, with great anticipation (and a slight degree of nervousness) for the jurors to announce their choice of the ten best manuscripts.

And that is how we were introduced to Keith Garebian, whose *Children of Ararat* was one of the ten books comprising Dektet 2010.

Children of Ararat dealt with the Armenian genocide of 1915. Generally forgotten by the world and actively denied and erased by the perpetrators, the desecration and horror were experienced by Keith through a lifetime spent processing the trauma of his father's stories of that genocide.

It is a relentless and powerful book, with eruptions of horror springing out of the simplest of images: a key scraping at an embankment reveals slivers of bone embedded in the clay; his father walks between rage and memory, "feet crimsoning the earth"; a swordsman straddles dismembered limbs.

As we prepared the manuscript it was manifest that Keith was someone who carried the burden of history constantly with him—indeed, not just *carried* it but had personally incorporated it, that he was expressing not only the weight and sorrow of his father's memories but had somehow embodied the memories and lives of all the victims. In a very real sense Keith as a poet had become a human arc for their stories and experiences, ferrying them through the great sea of indifference and forgetting and bringing their lives finally to shore, making them known to the world.

His book seemed packed with these souls, not just his own "murdered kin"—grandmother, grandfather, aunts, cousins—but all who had suffered "death by wholesale extraction": women taken from the public baths, children snatched from their schools, disappeared shopkeepers, the woman calling out to her child while stuffing vine leaves with rice and nuts, the grandmother whose remains fed the roots of a flowering plum tree, and those who had vanished from memory, the nameless ones of whom nothing remained but skeletal fragments, an eye socket, a bone sticking up through soil. All those lives that were never completed, never fully lived, and those too who survived, the countless orphans, children like his father who suffered without the comfort of those who might have relieved their suffering. He gathered them up as though he could somehow keep them all in memory until he could find justice for them.

It was of course gratifying that this understanding was felt not just by us as publishers of the book but was shared by so many insightful readers and critics: for example, Henry Beissel, "These poems are a splendid memorial which will continue to haunt the reader long after he has put them aside"; and Barry Callaghan, "Rage, for it to work on the page, requires a control so stern it seems like ease of phrase; historical pain made personal cannot be made convincing without such control and craft as is found in these poems by Keith Garebian"; or Jacob McArthur Mooney, in his review published in *The Globe and Mail*, "Garebian packs his story with the pure, corporeal horror that only a child can experience."

This collecting and carrying of souls is an innate part of Keith's life approach and poetic method, and is readily apparent in many of his other books. Lives collected and carried by him, the former wives and lovers, for example, who spill from the pages of *Finger to Finger*, and again in his collection i*n the bowl of my eye,* the many people who inhabit his environment: immigrants, the elderly, fellow condo dwellers, the ghosts of the indigenous who haunt the shores of the lake, and the white settlers who dislocated them—all those souls, some fulfilled, some not, some happily conspicuous, others scarcely seen, the whole flock gathered up and carried along to be finally released into the security of his poems.

This personal sensitivity is, of course, shared by many poets and is not unique to Keith Garebian, although very few, indeed, succeed in taking it to such an intense and finely etched level. In addition to this insight, there is another dimension to Garebian, which is an almost unique versatility combined with simply astonishing levels of output. A prime example is his biography of the Canadian actor William Hutt. *William Hutt: Soldier Actor* could serve as a master class in how to write biography: insightful, appreciative but without a trace of idolatry, near-perfect in style. Books of this quality generally take many years of research, then many more years to write and complete—but this title was completed (at least in comparative terms) practically overnight, all the time while the author was simultaneously producing his ongoing canon of poetry. Many times in reading this book we asked ourselves: how does he do this?

Or similarly, *Colours to the Chameleon,* a study of how actors develop and perfect their own understanding of Shakespeare. Or *The Making of Cabaret*, an historical and analytical study of how a Broadway play evolved from a set of short stories written decades earlier about the seemingly incompatible subjects of love and the rise of Nazi Germany.

And then—and almost antithetically—comes his astonishing small masterpiece, *Accidental Genius*, a deliberately wicked selection of out-of-context quotations accompanied by parodies of critical comment. The selections are perfect, the commentaries spot-on—altogether, one of the most amusing yet insightful political satires imaginable.

Over and over, reading these books, we were always confronted by the same questions: how does one writer develop such versatility; and how does he do this in such prodigious volume; and, most of all, how does he achieve all of these feats with such unfailing, uncompromising quality?

We can think of no other writer about whom we would more sincerely ask these questions than Keith Garebian.

Witness of the Past

Keith Garebian's *against forgetting*

MICHELINE MAYLOR

Keith Garebian's work is that of witness. Garebian has observed much in his long and robust life. His poems are a gold mine of history, human behaviour, and personal change. He observes and reveals worlds without sentimentality. I first encountered Keith's work while reading a long poem titled "Old Griefs" in which a father's entire being becomes revealed through portraiture of mixed heritage and a fraught life in Armenia tinted with sorrow before migrating to Canada. The close-up biography of the father with his superstitions and burdens revealed the character succinctly and clearly.

> His middle daughter's name meant gem.
> When she became gravely ill,
> He flung her pearl earrings away.
> The land had strange fits.
> Underground was close to hell.

Within a few stanzas I felt I knew Garebian's origin story and what he had to overcome as the son of a burdened man. What I came to know later about Garebian only furthered my respect for him and his personal resilience as I learned of his diagnosis of throat cancer and his late-in-life coming out story. He's a man of intense resilience despite losing his homeland and feeling 'other' for most of his life. Self-described as a "resident alien" and "Anglo-Indian," Garebian has found his place and identity through trauma by way of poetry and the language of the witness-narrator. Often telling a whole story in fragment or recollection, his vocabulary and imagery accumulate to startle, and more so, remind us of the near past. For the 20th century was a different era, one without personal technology, one where the rules and mores of society were more cleanly set behind traditions and limitations. It's here Keith becomes a conjurer, for his portraits stun with detailed accuracy. Here are a few lines from the opening of *against forgetting*:

My mother's plum velvet dress.
Her Tosca perfume. Her lipstick.
Father, younger than I am now,
in a botanical garden.
Marble statuary, two women.
Sometimes the faces are partial.
The necessary angle is wrong
to see the frame entirely. Accidental
bloom of shrubbery conceals.
Camera is mismanaged.

Garebian manages to encapsulate the entirety of the relationship of his parents through this pin-sharp setting and scene. It is only one example of his management of imagery through finely honed detail. We already know the tone and mood of his childhood: wrong, mismanaged, stiff, and a touch of sumptuous elegance.

While this purview encapsulates the tight relational sphere of family, Garebian's attention to societal mismanagement is also acute and affecting. As an immigrant, Garebian's assessment of political structures lacks any sense of nationalistic affiliation; it just reports on the atrocities and his attempts to aid.

In the 60s, I taught boat people,
whose adolescent minds couldn't shake off
sea water, rapacious rapists
and abductors who turned sunlight
blood-orange. Nor shake off the acrid
memory of smoke and flame floating
above jungle and valley.

What to teach those tormented
by fire and water, forever cursed
by booby traps ready to spring under
shattered stars, those who smuggle
broken selves which keep tunnelling
without reaching anything, except grief?

While stark, Garebian, taps into another time and place with a fusty attention, "a dying breed commemorated in Kipling." Of course, this history is relevant still and calls to mind lines from Warsan Shire's poem "Home." "No one leaves home unless / home is the mouth of a shark / you only run for the border / when you see the whole city running as well." Garebian turns back to look at the excavation of history and report on the results unflinchingly with such considerations as economics and race shifting.

Bhowani Junction: Mr. Jones, senior driver on the Delhi Deccan Railway,
married to a dark-skinned wife who chews betel nut in secret, encourages
her swarthy daughter Victoria to be "Spanish."
There was a young lady called Starkie
Who had an affair with a darkie.
The result of her sins

Was an eightsome of twins—
Two black and two white and four khaki.

Garebian's work pulls from a bygone era still steeped with relevance for the impulse to belong and what it means to be out of the centre of the dominant culture.

But in school, imitation was imperative
in writing. We copied of echoes,
in elegant murmurs, fastidious facsimiles,
morphing into literary mimics, eclectic
to a fault, adept at borrowing contours
and tones, without quite inventing our own.

At this stage of maturity, Garebian, is fully possessed of his own style and voice. He's a transformative writer who reveals other worlds and histories with the attentive language and cadence of a true poet. What Garebian teaches is how to belong in the here and now while pulling from a fragmented and broken past. He is not afraid to look at the ugliness of history and humanity in order to explore the humanity of one man doing his best to make sense of his experiences. Another of Garebian's books is titled *Poetry Is Blood.* This is relevant because he makes sense of his experiences and his identity through words and reflection. Poetry is a part of his most certain identity, the ground on which he stands. And we, as readers, can benefit from this inventory of history, family, and expression. Garebian finishes *against forgetting* through this final act of self-portraiture and reflection.

This self-portrait is a reflection
once removed. Words the glass,
unglazed, adhering to the face,
soul trying to break through

words to mirror hint of smile,
peculiar slant of memory,
inclinations of surfaces
enchantments of the self.

All is metaphor,
all is winding, leading to further windings,
all changing slightly, profoundly.

The past is here.

SCAN Cancer Poems

A Review

KEVIN IRIE

Breathe. Don't swallow. So starts the opening poem of Keith Garebian's chapbook *SCAN Cancer Poems* (Frog Hollow Press, 2021). It's an imperative voice, concise and direct, yet it is not the voice of Garebian himself but that of a medical worker giving him a scan, and immediately the reader is plunged head-first into Garebian's experience with throat cancer. In previous books, Garebian has notably dealt with the victims of politics (*Children of Ararat; Poetry Is Blood)* or with struggling artists (Frida Kahlo; Derek Jarman). Now his own physical struggle with forces beyond his control becomes his subject and, just as he has done before, Garebian bears witness:

> But I do not come in silence
> my words an intervention
> for undoing some things already done.

Note the tone: resolved, resolute, but realistic, all characteristic of these twenty extraordinary poems whose compressed complexity reveals more depth with each rereading and an amplification of Garebian's poetic themes. Yet coupled with this is an acknowledgement that, in the face of disease, poetry is not impervious, no matter how strong the voice.

> The self sustains itself
> on fallible words one by one
> But words cannot refuse

what's real:
death's heavier than syntax,
sonorous phrases,
structured images.

In *against forgetting* (2019), he wrote "I am a travelling swimmer, / in love with water." That comment seems ironic now with this chapbook's yearning imagery of the lake, swimming, and thirst. "Water, my element," Garebian writes here, but he is stranded like Prospero on his island, stranded in a hospital where patients are "diving into waters / they have not yet mastered," and conversation "swims slowly to life / in voices rasping, / gruff, wheezing."

In that same 2019 book, Garebian presciently wrote:

Long past middle age, I know
the dread of being swallowed
by something blue

Now the poems here describe his descent like an archetypal Jonah into the belly of a whale, a drowned, isolated world. References to friends, intimates, are mentioned but there is little contact recorded (which may well be due to weakened immunity) but this focuses and amplifies a sense of separation. Impressions, not narrative, not anecdotes, make up this collection, which makes it all the more compelling because we gain inner access into the poet's mind. "We are the voices of our present lives," Garebian wrote in 2019—and this present life is cancerous. The word "I" only appears in a fifth of the poems, in keeping with the sense that the body's cancer is the subject as much as the self-experiencing it. "I don't have a body / I am a body," he says, and these poems extend beyond the individual.

Art seeks not life but form, wrote Andre Aciman, and within this poetic suite, Garebian forms personal experience into literary art as he incorporates allusions to Freud, Goya, Nietzsche and Antigone. Line by line, one notices how such links are made seamlessly, yet surely artfully, as a testament to Garebian's skills as a poet and an intellectual; how easily he can draw these references into his poems as natural spontaneous thoughts, not laboured connections.

Such illness defies Common Sense,
is shameful for some—
passion repressed or punished—
as in Freud's jaw cancer
gnawing body and psyche.

He quotes W.H. Auden, William Carlos Williams and Barry Dempster (in the moving poem "Glosa: Hope, This Skin") but one unspoken poetic connection is that of Orpheus after his head was torn off by the Maenads and cast into the River Hebron. Like Orpheus, Garebian is cast into a world swirling around him that he cannot control. But still he sings. And the poems sing in many voices: sad, contemplative, philosophical, acerbic. In "I Am a Body," he uses medical terminology in irreverent defiance:

extracapsular extension
(like a gym exercise?)
PET scan
(sounds like a benign pat on the head) ...

osteophyte fibrosis
(are we in the dead-zone already?)

Other times, he is lyrical, as in "Swimmable Sea":

Count the days where health
clears the room of sickness,
stopping the metaphorical octopus
from spreading its tentacles.
Sleep is now a swimmable sea.

Though Garebian has previously stated he is averse to "imitating Mary Oliver" (*in the bowl of my eye*, 2022), the poems here turn to Nature as a constant point of reference, no notebook in hand but still noted, as in "A Different Tolling Bell":

Morning fog has returned
after last week's false
lurch towards spring.
The park is a white silence
awakening to sounds

Yet his poetic style reveals a confidence: statements are made: metaphors are frequent, similes less so, as if to say this is the way it is, reflecting how certain Garebian is in how he sees the world.

A tugging animal in my throat:
cancer a predator out of his cage. Sirens sound
inside the body.

These lines are from the closing poem of Garebian's book *Finger to Finger*, published by Frontenac House in 2022, yet *SCAN Cancer Poems* had already been published in 2021. The reader can thus assume this is experience viewed in retrospect, offering some hope, not despair, for within this chapbook there is a world out of control, under duress, under the diagnosis of cancer. For the hospital patient, "the blue gown is not a celebration," and this is a masque of the red death recorded in an amazing feat of poetic legerdemain. As *SCAN Cancer Poems* encapsulates Garebian's recurring themes, a quote from an earlier book can summarize the spirit of this one. In "Antitheses," a poem about the self's opposing attitudes from *Poetry Is Blood* (2018), he wrote "One names a disease; / the other refuses to be it." Garebian has refused, and poetry is stronger for it.

Stranger from a Vanished Land

Keith Garebian's Father-Son Poetry

BRIAN BARTLETT

1. Two Fathers

On the first day of summer I relax in the cool shade of my family's Halifax backyard and reread Keith Garebian's poetry and prose rooted in memories of his father. At a glass table I eat a MacIntosh apple while delving into the poem "Okra" (PB 22-23). Garebian's tastes in food marked only one difference between him and his father; if family tensions hadn't been so pressing, the poem implies, "I would have shared my father's love for okra." To appreciate that poem more fully, should I buy and taste okra for the first time? That question might be a comical prompting to feel from a poem—yet why shouldn't our reading expand our palate, literally as well as metaphorically? A more significant expansion: language imaginatively taking us into lives distant from our own. I'm wondering about the taste of okra; the next moment I'm jotting down notes that Adam Garebian was born in December 1909 (or 1910—passports and a marriage license differ on that matter) and died in December 1995.

An essential key Keith Garebian uses in trying to understand his father is the raw fact that Adam (in Armenian, Atam) was a child in 1915 during the genocidal massacre of over a million Armenians: "Blood becoming rivers, / souls of the dead that never saw me. / My father comes from that deluge" (AF 34). Since my father died in early June only four years ago, a few months before his 94th birthday, he's been on my mind during my reading of works by Adam's son. Adam Garebian and Lester Bartlett were radically different men. In his son's memories, the former was scarred and traumatized, detached and confrontational, with "angry basilisk eyes" (AF 56) and an "adamantine will" (CA 20). The son has published a poem called "His Roaring"" (CA 20-23); one reason for the father's loudness was his years working in a "cacophonous factory," where "workers thickened the air with curses, / machinery clanged," but his roaring also grew out of his conviction that "nothing / would make his life / holy and right again." Adam's son recalls a childhood time when "I thought / for a while he was the strongest man / in the world, who could tame the sea" (CA 93). (The qualifiers "I thought" and "for a while" hint at both the son's naiveté and the father's weaknesses and vulnerabilities.) In brooding moods, Adam drank "whiskey and soda, gin, beer, / and something called *hootch* / fermented in rubber bladders" (CA 22). His son suggests that some of his self-assured, stubborn efforts to dominate dinnertime conversation stemmed from his having been "so vilely deprived of a formal education" (PS 2).

My father was too gentle a man for his children to imagine him as a Poseidon taking charge of the sea. I never heard him shout or roar, nor did I ever know him to touch an alcoholic drink. He and his eight siblings were all (as far as I know) teetotallers, in part because an uncle of theirs had suffered from excessive drinking. My father had university degrees in science and education. He carefully avoided confrontation (which resulted in the build-up of inner anxieties during his later career as a civil-service manager). The family at large knew him for his wide, warm smile. Garebian writes in one poem about Adam's earliest years, "Photos of young Armenian orphans provoked my hunger for his boyhood face" (PB 74), whereas I have many photos of my father in his youth; and while Garebian never met his paternal grandparents—both dead before his birth—and has never seen photos of them, I had dozens of visits and meals with my grandparents over many years, and value photos mirroring moments in their lives from nine decades of the twentieth century. Another fundamental difference between Adam Garebian and my father was historical and cultural: My father grew up in rural New Brunswick, Canada, in an essentially sheltered, peaceful environment, with two parents who would live long lives, along with many brothers and sisters, and he never faced violent oppression or subsequent emotional, mental scarring from childhood horrors spread across a whole culture.

This unconventional autobiographical introduction to a discussion of poetry grows out of feelings of gratitude for Keith Garebian's ongoing, many-faceted writings about a father he found difficult in life yet worthy of a son's most compassionate understanding. Just as Adam was haunted by his father (who was "suddenly 'recruited' into the Turkish army and disappeared forever in a convoy to the front—PS 3), Keith in turn is haunted by the haunted father. With its sharp etching of dramatic moments and its precise musings on a man's harshly shadowed life, the poetry reveals to us both Adam's experiences and the son's efforts to know his father better. The gratitude I feel is also for the opportunity to appreciate anew the fortunate childhood and adult years my father knew, and to listen carefully to a different son's unsparingly honest words about his different, deeply troubled father.

2. Talking of and to

During the past quarter of a century Canadian writers have wrestled in words with father-child relationships more than during any previous period. Memorable nonfiction books in that vein have included *Miriam* Toews's *Swing: A Low Life*

(1998), Rachel Manley's *In My Father's Shade* (2004), Elizabeth Hay's *All Things Consoled: A Daughter's Memory* (2018), Mark Abley's *The Organist: Fugues, Fatherhood and a Fragile Mind* (2019) and David Macfarlane's *Likeness: Fathers, Sons, a Portrait.* (2021). A handful of our twenty-first-century poets have also written not just once or twice but repeatedly about having or being fathers (e.g. Richard Harrison, Shane Neilson, Julie Bruck). Recalling the powerful presence of fatherhood in recent Canadian poetry and nonfiction (not to exclude fiction) provides a broad context for exploring Garebian's writings that draw upon memories of his father. A book could be written examining the subject as addressed by writers of our country during this century, including connections between them and writers from other countries and continents.

Much of the time Garebian speaks of his father in third-person, but occasionally he adopts a "you" and addresses the most important male in his past. Speaking to Adam, Garebian writes:

> ... your voice has not gone.
> I carry it in my head
> as I write this poem
> about a dead man
> whose every second thought was of death. (CA 20)

The survival of a deceased parent's voice in a child's memory is familiar to us from living and reading; but in the lines just quoted Garebian speaks with rare directness, and he makes a striking shift moving from father as "you" to "a dead man / whose every second thought was of death." That shift might be a means to combine directness with a poet's admission that poetry sometimes asks a "you" to become a generalized figure transcending the specific and the personal. In reading those lines I don't forget that Keith Garebian is speaking not only *of* but also *to* his father, but I also sense an allusion to countless people throughout history—especially many Armenians deeply traumatized by 1915—who lived every day with thoughts of death's reality and proximity.

One brief Garebian poem of son addressing father is simply entitled "I Have Inherited You" (CA 29). That title, doubling as the poem's first line, defamiliarizes *inheritance*, which usually suggests the passing on of land, money or objects. To speak of inheriting a father—moreover, in words directed at the deceased father—is a complex act. What the son receives isn't heirlooms or a certain number of acres but, more drastically and mysteriously, the father himself. The poem's second and third lines read: "your voice in my head / a pressure, a haunting / what will outlast me, / unless I heed it." Listening to the father, then, is seen as depressurizing, and as crucial for giving hope that the father's haunting doesn't continue even after the son's death. This isn't the only time that Garebian alludes to a kind of responsibility he feels to keep bringing his father's memories into the present. Another poem suggests one role the poet has taken on: "My father's people vanished into nothing / and I reach into the corners of night / to guess where their spirits may pass" (PB 49). Despite knowing that his labours will be limited by vanishings and guesswork, the poet feels compelled to make written afterlives for both the father and his people.

In two consecutive poems in the collection *Children of Ararat*, "The Plum Tree" and "Flotsam" (16-17), Garebian address his father about his grandmother (Adam's mother). The first poem contrasts images of the title tree, "its fruit bent low with sweetness," and of a moon "gliding softly in a silver loop," with the unrest and violence plaguing the woman the poet would never have a chance to meet: "Your mother's life bent and broken," "Your mother screaming as an axe smashed doors" and, concluding the poem, "your mother's blood feeding [the plum tree's] roots." While the tree "stands where it always stood," Adam's mother's walking on the earth ended tragically soon. In "Flotsam," Garebian imagines his father in childhood ("She was lost in your sobbing, noon / prickling your boyish mind"), and a subsequent time (vaguely given as "Later") when "you would learn she was lifted into a cart, / dumped into a ravine, her face dissolving / in the crimson river's current." As in the previous poem, Garebian concentrates on his father's experiences rather than on his own inability to have ever known the woman. Neither poem speaks of "my grandmother"; Garebian's sympathy is with his forever-grieving father—though a close reading of the poems needs to acknowledge the sad gap created in the poet's life.

3. More than an Archetype

While some poets write about their fathers mostly in archetypical terms, refraining from fleshing-out with everyday details—so the father emerges more generalized and representative than individual—in his poetry Keith Garebian presents his father as a man revealed in many dramatic situations and scenes, and in repeated consideration of his cultural roots. In his poetry the son gives the father a fragmentary biography.

Garebian is aware that terse reductions of lives and persons risk great sacrifices of accuracy and thoroughness. "Each of us is never a single world," he writes in "How I Was Made" (AF 21); then, with appealing hyperbole: "Whole islands, cities, countries, / continents, exist in us." No biography is complete without investigating the subject's parentage and original cultural context. In both prose and poetry Garebian has touched on his family's name. In "Okra": "Our family name is from Arabic. Gareb— / from the land of strangers. Or simply stranger." From another poem: "My father, truly *gharib*, outsider, / stranger from a vanished land" (AF 34). More recently, in *Pieces of My Self: Fragments of an Autobiography*, Garebian's prose opens into even greater elaborateness about the family name: "... it derives from a Turkish-Arabic word for 'stranger' or sometimes 'pilgrim': *garip* or *gharib*. It is a word with many radiations of meaning: comical, extraordinary, fantastic, grotesque, peculiar, quaint, queer, quirky, strange. Many of these adjectives are applicable to my own and my father's life" (16-17). The multiplicity of meanings for the root of *Garebian* branches into the multiple transformations in the lives of father and son.

The breadth of scenes Garebian sketches of his father's life is unusually wide, ranging from his childhood time in an orphanage with a cousin ("they sailed in a makeshift raft, / got caught. Armenian Tom and Huck"—PB 17) to his death of cancer in an Ontario hospital (his mouth "a small black hole, caught / with grotesque suddenness / in the rigor mortis of unspoken / havoc"—CA 93). While some poets write for a concentrated time about a parent, Garebian is a rare poet (think also of Sharon Olds) repeatedly writing of his father in poetry spanning many years. An essay should also be written about Garebian's writings on his mother. While his father belonged to "the ravaged side / of my family" (CA 22), and was full of fury and confusion, "My Anglo-Indian mother was sweet, gentle, patient, diplomatic" (PS 21). Armenia was the country with the most profound effect on Adam Garebian, though he lived, married and became a father in India; a poem by his son refers to Bombay as "named / after Great Mother, *Maha Amba*" (AF 21). Surely much of the satisfaction and belonging that Adam knew stemmed partly from his marriage. The third major stage of Adam's life began with his move to Canada, a month before his son's eighteenth birthday. The great majority of the poetry's most vividly sketched moments from the father's life and of the most emotionally crucial reflections on the father connect to his Asian beginnings; despite the many subsequent years spent in Canada, the experiences most burned into Adam's memory transpired in Armenia and India. In a poem concerning the family's new life in Canada, Garebian writes: "I am safe in my second country, except / in what I am condemned to remember" (AF 48). With "third" substituted for "second," those words could have been spoken by the father Adam.

4. The Father in the Son

Garebian makes no bones about the many tensions between him and his father. One poem begins, "So rare was his warm touch on my head or skin / I cannot remember it" (CA 93), and another is open-heartedly titled, "My Father and I Rarely Touched" (PB 74). Elsewhere, Keith sums up distant Adam's argumentative tendencies and the alienation between father and son this way: "The old father, to whom I was never close, / wanted his epitaph to read On the contrary" (PB 84). A fourth poem opens with the mythic comparison "My father an Odysseus," and speaks of his wanderings happening "on his side of the wall built / by himself, by an army / of shadows hidden in crannies / far from olive trees and cypresses" (CA 15). Here the poet sees the wall dividing father from son as basically the father's doing, though in other poems he acknowledges his own contributions to the reticence. To call upon "Okra" again (PB 32-33): though the poet says, "I was searching for his heart but he never knew," he also admits that in his clash-prone dealings with his father, "I wanted to speak words / that were hurtful. / Nothing to do with okra." If readers of Garebian's poetry search for other dramas and descriptions of the father-son differences, they would do well to consult the first chapter of *Pieces of My Self*, in which Keith goes as far as to describe Adam and himself as "spiritual adversaries" (2).

Despite all the struggles between the two men, some of the most emotional moments in Garebian's father-son writings see them not as utterly alien from each other but as joined through shared needs, especially those to remember the past. One of the most affective, beautiful passages in Garebian's memoir reads: "I am my father's son, a stranger to his language and some of his countrymen's customs but an Armenian with eyes that sometimes have a deep-sea sadness and a soul across which the snows of Ararat blow: (18). "A Pilgrimage" (PB 61-63) includes the lines: "I walk in my orphaned / father's shoes, their footfall / imprinting his voicelessness." Synaesthesia links the sight of imprinted shoes with the sound (or soundlessness) of voicelessness. In a paradox found in this poem, the silence is between father and son: "Words between us were / silence disguised." Garebian's poem "Dektets in Homage" might be written partly in honour of his damaged father, yet it also includes striking lines of self-description: "Do you think I am talking only of my father's orphaned life? / It is I who am now trapped in an abyss" (CA 33). The title of another poem, "Nomad: Addressed to My Father and Myself" (CA 26), strikingly indicates that Adam and Keith share enough to be addressed simultaneously; the poem creates a complicated effect, in that each time the pronoun "you" appears it can refer to both father and son.

In being a poet, as his father wasn't, Garebian puts into reflective words some of the sentiments and griefs that his father found it hard to articulate without anxiety and anger. (Not that Garebian refrains from voicing his own anger; check out "I, Who Have Not Ascended Ararat," with lines like "in every Turkish history book, in every / school where revisionism is the new barbarity / (second genocide), inject Armenian blood"—CA 92). Near the end of "Dektets in Homage," Garebian writes: "These words supplement what my father remembered"

(CA 35). Another poem says outright, “We need elegies, need history,” and elaborates:

> ... there is a closeness with these dead
> and an extravagance, my displacement
> out of their time and place.
> I consign myself to night
> and the collective dead
> who remain unnamed ... (PB 49)

In that passage, Garebian expresses his taking on the role of elegiac poet. While he knows he is at a remove from the slaughtered Armenians of his father’s and grandparents’ generations, as the son of a young survivor he insists on remembering what he didn’t personally go through. The “extravagance” he speaks of could be the gap between 1915 and the early 21st-century, as well his claim to have “closeness” to the unnamed victims. “I consign myself to ... / ... the collective dead” is one of Garebian’s most explicit declarations of one basic dimension of his poetry, one grounded in the forces that wounded his father.

Another poem that outwardly expresses elegiac needs and intentions is simply called “Elegy” (PB 89-91). It begins with a stanza that self-reflexively cites the site and act of writing: “My father’s ancient tribe writhes / on my written page, / groaning under a sullen sun. One reason “Elegy” is superior to the poem preceding it, “Reducible” (PB 88), is that the earlier poem is weighed down with words like “madness,” “lamentation,” “terror,” “Hysteria,” “pain” and “outage,” while the following poem offers the immediacy of a speaking “I” and the imagery of fruits, flowers, playing children and “wild red rivers.” Once again, a kind of extravagance, of going beyond normal bounds of speech, is achieved and welcome: Garebian imagines his ancestors writhing on the page, then in the second stanza he writes, "I speak of myself when I speak of them, / my perennial hallucination / of death's pandemonium" (the two multi-syllabic line-ending words echoing off each other). Closer to the end of the poem Garebian writes, "I shelter the dead, / given them refuge in my words." Though "Elegy" nowhere uses the word "father," the profound task it outlines is one inherently connected to Adam Garebian.

If the poet Garebian sometimes leaves his father's traumatized memories of 1915 unstated in poems about the Armenian tragedy, he also frequently imagines his father at the center of imagined events. For a couple of readings, I mistakenly thought that one of those events appears in "Discovery" (11-12), the first poem of the collection *Children of Ararat*, whose first part is entitled "Adam." The horrific details that begin the book, of fallen-out eyes and teeth "set in clay / wall of a hill in northern Syria," lead into a nightmarish image of a man I assumed to be the father (who could also be the poet son, despite the section title) digging into clay with car keys, finding skulls "collapsing into paste / as the wet air touches / calcium for the first time / since a thousand bodies / disappeared." I initially read the poem as a no-holds-barred fantasy of the father digging into his cultural past. Only weeks after first poring over the poem did I read in the "Notes" at the collection's back that the poem's discovery was inspired by those of two journalists and another individual whom Garebian's note identifies by name. But I've decided to share my misreading here, as an illuminating case of a poem having a life independent of its sources and its author's intentions. In the context of Garebian's many poems delving into his father's life, the (mis)reading appropriately imagines Adam finding decayed remains of his people's past in all their tangibility and odour.

How much does the honouring, remembering poet help *create* the father presented in the poems? Garebian is self-aware enough as a poet, and as a person, to at least hint that the father presented is inevitably imagined, not only recalled. This allows Keith to write long after Adam's death: "... he has grown / in me as I stir memory's water." The act of stirring water suggests a kind of conjuring—but a conjuring grounded very much in trying to achieve as accurate as possible a recollection and portrait of a man as he was.

5. A Strand Digression

Two decades before I first read Keith Garebian's poetry, I read and taught Mark Strand's "Elegy for My Father," and listened a few times to a recording of the poet reading sections of the long multi-part poem. When I recently re-encountered the poem, one passage of it in particular resonated with Garebian's elegiac poetry for his father:

> Your clothes carried your shadow inside; when you took them off, it
> spread like the dark of your past.
> And your words that float like leaves in an air that is lost, in a place
> no one knows, gave you back your shadow.
> Your friends gave you back your shadow.
> Your enemies gave you back your shadow. They said it was heavy
> and would cover your grave.
>
> (139)

From now on it might be difficult for me to re-read Strand's poem without being reminded of Garebian's; or some of the Armenian-Canadian poet's lines, without thinking of the Canadian-born American poet. Thus, in one reader's experiences do poems speak to each other across great—or not-so-great—distances.

6. Sons' Synchronicity

On a concluding personal note, about apt, pleasing synchronicity:

Embarking on an exploration of Keith Garebian's son-father poetry, I had already written several drafts of a long eight-part poem, "Our Father in His Nineties." Then, several months ago, the literary journal *The Antigonish Review* accepted three sections of the poem for publication in their winter issue. What a surprise it was later to discover that the same issue would include several Garebian poems that further meditated on his bonds with his father and his mother. I await the arrival of that issue, which will bring into closer proximity two fathers as dissimilar as Adam Garebian and Lester Bartlett. Meanwhile, a few lines by Garebian could powerfully serve as a statement for many poets writing of their fathers. Here "imagined" doesn't suggest made up from scratch; it means recorded carefully and faithfully: "I root my father in an imagined place, / loved without judgement. / I give his ghost ascendancy. He will not be erased" (AB 76).

Sources

Books by Keith Garebian referred to in this essay include—with abbreviations given here in bold—*Children of Ararat* (Frontenac House, 2010) CA; *Poetry Is Blood* (Guernica Editions, 2018) PB; *against forgetting* (Frontenac House, 2019) AF; *Pieces of My Self: Fragments of an Autobiography* (Guernica Editions, Miroland, 2023) PS. The lines by Mark Strand appear in his *Collected Poems* (Knopf, 2014), but were originally in *The Story of Our Lives* (1973).

Regarding Keith Garebian

GEORGE ELLIOTT CLARKE

Keith Garebian (1943-) is a belle-lettrist who comes to poetry only *via* deadly and difficult histories arising from his dual heritage: Armenian patrilineal; Anglo-Indian matrilineal. His father survived the 1915-1917 genocide that Turks visited upon Armenians (but that the once-Ottomans deny ever happened); his mother preferred to be English—the despotic masters of colonial India—though her home was India, a nation belonging to Indians, the subjugated, reviled, and restive "natives." Thus, the young poet matured in a household haunted by the father's unspeakable witness of mass slaughter committed by a government that fibs about wrongdoing and scoffs at guilt; but also one in which his mother saw no need for a rapprochement between her Anglo privilege and her Indian "indigeneity." Added to these fissures or dilemmas in the developing poet's psyche were his alienation from his silently suffering survivor's guilt, self-medicating-with-alcohol father and then his remote mother become even more remote due to her premature death; as well as his own sexuality which was *prima facie* "het"; I mean, merely superficially "het." His late poem, "Anglo-India," published in *against forgetting* (2019)[1], spells out the tempestuous, family drama of his boyhood:

> Father, displaced Armenian, reinvented
> as waiter and automobile mechanic
> in the Persian Gulf, then Works Manager
> of French Motors, British-owned Bombay company,
> whose executives visited
> like imperial tourists, absentee landlords.

> Mother, [...]
> Never curious about bastard history,
> tale of a tribe adrift or resigned
> to rejection by India and Britain,
> one contempt redounding on another. (26)

Domestic comfort played out, cheek-by-jowl, with irrepressible, funky destitution, the "Chaos of bastard styles [of architecture], grotesquely / comic colonial legacy" plunked among huts with cow-dung-matted doorways, all helping to establish "how beauty can push through poverty of means" (*against* 22). His bourgeois household's ruling-class camouflage dispatched Garebian to a boys-only school, Jesuitical, yes, but also dumbly hypocritical about "Sex." In a land where hawks cry "in mid-air copulations" (23) and "temples bore sculptures of holy men / praying beneath a gigantic vulva," how could his Catholic teachers not become "sex demonic" (30). En route to becoming a man, the boy nursed on cleavages, *cauchemars*, inhibitions, prohibitions, all the seismic, psychic shifts, shudders, quivers, and faults that manifest a poet.

Originally, though, Garebian was—in terms of publication—a man-of-letters, just as he was, at first, heterosexual, even through two marriages and siring a son. As of 2022, his 26 books number only eight poetry titles (not including his chapbook, *SCAN Cancer Poems* [2021])[2]. After completing and publishing his dissertation on Canadian novelist Hugh Hood[3], Garebian found a lucrative and unique, scholarly vein to mine, authoring books on the "making of" major Broadway musicals, including *West Side Story*, *Cabaret*, *My Fair Lady*, *Gypsy*, and *My Fair Lady*. Among these popular titles are his biography of the formidable, Canadian actor William Hutt, a study of playwright George Bernard Shaw and his stage interpreter Christopher Newton, plus scrutiny of Canadian novelist

Leon Rooke, and interviews with Canadian actors musing on Shakespeare and productions of his plays.[4] Although he taught at McGill and Concordia universities, and was a perennial lecturer at Trent University, Garebian never became an Ivory Tower inmate—with tenure and sunshine-list salary—and so, he sought to pay his bills by writing consummately literate and empathetic but clear-eyed theatre reviews for a host of newspapers, magazines, websites, and journals. Indeed, besides being a perennial recipient of "most outstanding" and "*magnum cum laude*" academic awards, his first major literary notice was as a runner-up for the 1982 Nathan Cohen Award for Outstanding Theatre Criticism.[5] His first prominence—and eminence—then is as a theatre critic, and likely the dominant figure in this capacity since Nathan Cohen shuttered his typewriter with his 1971 decease. One may also surmise that the turn to penning the literature of the theatre was a way for Garebian to appreciate the artistry of Queer actors, playwrights, and directors, thereby allowing himself to accept his own (once-repressed) sexual orientation.

I am moved to this consideration given that Garebian's third poetry tome, *Blue: The Derek Jarman Poems* (2008),[6] edited by the fine (Queer) poet John Barton, is a meditation on the life of Jarman (1942-1994)—"filmmaker, visual artist, poet, sexual rebel, and a gardener" (back cover). Garebian is classed as "an insatiable cinéaste" (back cover), but I believe that he wished to ponder and "reanimate" Jarman due to his status as a Briton pursuing same-sex relationships in an era when it was still *Verboten* in blunt High Church and Tory commandments. In newly independent India, Garebian's exposure to the print pornography available to a schoolboy,[7] had fed fantasies of "elegant Sodoms in the garden of England— / naked guardsmen running through bushes / and middle-aged men rushing to the arms / of vacant-eyed boys" (*Blue* 11). Also attractive to

Garebian is Jarman's up-yours ripostes to his mildly homophobic father and the disgusting, anti-Gay prejudice of the shabby England of the 1950s:

> You told of pain—betrayals,
> admonitions, millennia of Christian hatred,
> a hurtful God to kill childhood
> in bells and sermons, threats of hell fire,
> the sacred warfare of a weird tribe.
> You vowed rebellion—shedding of the veil
> of matrimony, fucking of the groom
> and wiping up with the Saviour's shroud. (12)

Something there is about "Blasphemy" that requires "Buggery" (33), eh? The once-Catholic schoolboy Garebian is thrilled to encounter, in Jarman's multiple arts, the provocative thesis that "Every time you read ancient history, / you saw the heart of a dangerous love"; i.e., that "All civilization [is] a queer history" (12). Like Negrophobes whiting out Black history, so must homophobes obscure, obliterate, and opaque (out) the history of Queer civilizing of heterosexual-dominated factions (groupings not yet civilizations). In drafting his verse-bio of Jarman, Garebian also embraces a host of other Queer cultural icons: Caravaggio, Ginsberg, Pasolini, Genet, Fassbinder, St. Sebastian, Cocteau, Edward II, Wittgenstein. Several of these figures were murdered (or martyred); then again, even "Jesus is gay" (34). In the brief prose bio at the book's back, one reads that Jarman "first experienced sex with another boy at boarding school" (105): Was this detail the first point of conjunction between poet and subject? Of course, I can't say; what I can say is that *Blue: The Derek Jarman Poems* is a glorious, painterly palette of Jarman; of unorthodox art as the product of a subterranean, yet subversive subculture; of highlighting same-sex lovers as the quintessential civilizers of otherwise barbaric cultures. Also notable here is Garebian's fetishizing of the colour *blue*:

> blue remains a hard diamond.
> The blue tattoos of boys in Venice,
> the blue of sad-eyed lethargy;
> indigo night on gypsy faces
> and a sapphire sea.
> Blue was the colour of your skin
> at the end of your garden ... (13)

Blue—the colour—shows up everywhere in Garebian's poetry[8]; and it may be that it signals the beautiful and the perilous, the authoritative cerulean of sky and sea, the sapphire or indigo melanin of mixed-race persons (but more "white" than dark-complected), and, simultaneously, the seventh heaven of artistic achievement (which is not to be confused with heaping up capital and capturing *beaucoup* prizes), but with winning to *sui generis* (and generous) genius. Then again, the references to colour by any racialized minority subject (and Garebian's apportion of melanin grants him a tan complexion) are never innocent. Assuredly, as I theorize elsewhere, "racialized subjects—especially intellectuals—demonstrate a hypersensitivity to colour for it defines, or they let it define, a signal portion of their consciousness" (Clarke 63). I continue on to state the following:

> Given that "colour" is used as racial metaphor, it is natural that a "black" person might look askance at "whiteness" (such as the clichéd bedsheet-robes of the Ku Klux Klan, or, for that matter, the Disneyfied paleness of *Snow White*) or celebrate blackness (in clothes, in ink, in coffee, etc.), partly so as to counteract the

> negativity that Western civilization sights in sombre shades. But it is practically inevitable that the intellectual "of colour" will consider all tints in terms of their symbolic import. They—I mean, we—are *never* colour-blind.[9]

Garebian's fetishization of *blue* must indicate racial, sexual, and even migratory (crossing the blue ocean to Canada) traumas or complexes of emotionally urgent coloratura.

My first encounter with Garebian as a reviewer of his books was my assessment of *Georgia and Alfred* (2015),[10] which *likely* appeared in the Halifax (NS) Herald newspapers (*The Chronicle-Herald* and/or *The Mail-Star*) on Monday, November 23, 2015, under this headline: "Clarke: Garebian's art forays hit-and-miss." *Georgia and Alfred* is another biographical inquiry, examining the aesthetics and sex ethics of Georgia O'Keeffe (1887-1986) and Alfred Stieglitz (1864-1946) as pioneering US artists in their different media—and as a sensual couple, with O'Keeffe serving as Stieglitz's model or muse. Having now twice-read *Georgia and Alfred*, I will quote from my original review:

> Garebian's free verse format is anchored by footnotes and fleshed out with found poems gleaned from real-life letters or biographies or critics' second thoughts. The lyrics are as documentary as they are confessional.
>
> O'Keeffe's "found" lines are sometimes painterly: "charcoal—[is] a miserable medium / for things that seem alive / and sing"; "Stem and leaf ... / sheens of shape / have subtle possibilities for my brush / Words would guillotine them."
>
> Stieglitz's "found" lines are functional to the point of being perfunctory: "All lived moments are equally true, / equally important."
>
> The poetry is most vivid when Garebian isn't documenting, but trying to sketch—or snap—the inner lives of his subjects as lovers and/or artists:

> "Camera Work" has us glimpse Stieglitz thinking, "Say platinum, gum bichromate, Carbon, etc. / light an economy of mood / shadow its imprint."[11]
>
> The love affair is neatly pictured: "In high summer her shanty / studio is glutted with apples. // Their shine fills trees all morning, / burdened boughs straining / with the weight of this light / that falls on her nakedness [posed for him] like fever."[12]
>
> Roughly 2/3 of the poems deal with Stieglitz looking at O'Keeffe and snapping her or other models, to conclude that males are fixated on coitus and/or the eternal feminine.[13] Is this news?
>
> O'Keeffe focuses on Nature: "Shingle dissolves into leaf, / and the shell is a white memory. / Shining praise for the design in things."[14]
>
> Fine lines are found in this collection, along with some—including the "found poems"—that are just pedestrian.
>
> More grit and sparks might have appeared had Garebian explored the illicit love between O'Keeffe and another artist, the African-American poet Jean Toomer [1894-1967].

I stand by the mild chiding that I express above regarding Garebian's tendency to overly rely on what he presumes to be the spontaneous, natural poetry voiced or writ by artistic greats. However, deathless painters and photographers may not be—and, in this book, are not—equally talented at literary expression.[15] The thesis expounded herein is that males (whether artists or not) have a tendency to want to pour their "strains" (Africadian slang for *semen*) into as many (accepting) niches, crevices, or "pockets" as possible, and woe unto those Puritans who would try to put the kibosh on wantons (and nymphos). Art will out—and cocks-o-the-walk will "come out" for male and/or female rendezvous—irrepressibly and incessantly.

In any event, as is the case in *Blue: The Derek Jarman Poems*, *blue* is again significant in *Georgia and Alfred*. One lyric, "Blue Is a Hole,"[16] reviews the tint:

> blue is a hole in the bone
> the blue which comes
> from holding the hole to the sky
> the sky that is more
> than bone in one's world. (*Georgia* 75)

Although I have listed several possible ramifications for the "apparition" of this tint throughout Garebian's oeuvre, it likely has the same sexual-psycho import for Garebian as he believes it does (or did) for Jarman: "The landscape of your heart's / blue is austere ..."; "O blue, your body chimes / with admirable longings ..." (*Jarman* 101).

Art, homosexuality lived among heterosexual opprobrium, and genealogy-as-destiny are Garebian's triadic concerns. For me, the latter interest occasions his most persuasive, his most "must-read," his most compelling work. So, let us turn now to *Children of Ararat* (2010).[17] Dedicated to Garebian's father, Adam (1909-1995), the book retraces initial forays into the subject matter—the Turkish extermination (attempted) of Armenians, 1915-1917—in Garebian's first memoir, *Pain: Journeys Around My Parents* (2000)[18] as well as in his first book of poems, *Reservoir of Ancestors* (2003)[19]. However, it is also painfully, poignantly, an all-new record of "the horror that is too often the result of politics and too much the truth of history."[20] Although blurbs are often singularly unreliable as a means to gauge a book's excellence, *Children of Ararat* arrived with back-cover endorsements from Armenian-American poet Peter Balakian, Canadian poet and publisher Barry Callaghan, as well as from Japanese-Canadian author Joy Kogawa, herself a survivor of the racist internment of Japanese-Canadians during World War II. Such literal "backing" (excuse the pun) cannot be ignored.

Garebian begins, as he must, with his father, who "swallows all / he can of desecration" (*Children* 12); i.e., the suggestion that he is lying when he recalls "A cemetery where your mother disappeared before / you could return with water to soothe her blistered lips. / ... Later you would learn she was lifted into a cart, / dumped into a ravine, her face dissolving / in the crimson river's current, her body / a floating shadow amid cruising fish" (17). Horror *partout*; horror infecting even nature: "The plum tree stands where it always stood. And your mother's blood feeding the roots" (16). I must observe—while banishing any suggestion of the trite—that Garebian was born to write these poems. He is himself a type of Hamlet, reiterating the tragic hero's anxious recognition: "The time is out of joint. Oh, cursed spite, / That ever I was born to set it right!" (Hamlet I.v.195-196.) Garebian's father has been discombobulated, disoriented, because he has been disabused of the notion that there is any sublunary, secular justice. "Thirst" is a primer to Adam's alcoholism; yet, "What swam in his blood / was more than alcohol—a debt / he felt unable to pay to ancestors / trapped in a desert's stench of death..." (22); thus, he got drunk and roared "for remembered wreckage" (23). Worse, just as the prose poem "Blood Memory" relates, Adam Garebian "almost killed a young Muslim who had insulted Christians": He "almost drowned the victim in a tank of water, blood memory rushing to his brain" (28). "He almost killed, in consideration of his murdered kin" (28). Luckily, other workers intervened and the head-dunked man was saved. And that's just for starters! *Children of Ararat* also narrates the son Garebian's journey to Armenia, a tourism that is a flashback to terrorism: "how this mother with the bayonet inside her,

/ would have loved this baby in her belly…" (49). Although Garebian's talents can falter in other books, *Children of Ararat* is an epochal triumph, no matter what else he writes—or has written. (Garebian's follow-up to *Children of Ararat*, namely, *Poetry Is Blood*,[21] is also stellar.)

Keith Garebian has read everyone, from Anne Carson to Michael Ondaatje, not to mention Billyum Shakespeare. Still, to me, he seems closest to the Turkish Communist poet, Nazim Hikmet, as well as to the Greco-Egyptian—and Queer—Nobel Laureate in Literature C.P. Cavafy. Place now his star among the aurora borealis.

Notes

1. Keith Garebian, *against forgetting* (Calgary: Frontenac House Poetry, 2022).
2. Keith Garebian, *SCAN Cancer Poems* (Victoria, BC: Frog Hollow Press, 2022).
3. Keith Garebian, *Hugh Hood and His Works* (Toronto: ECW Press, 1985). Garebian's first book on Hood, entitled *Hugh Hood*, appeared as part of Twayne's Author Series (1983).
4. Although I checked several websites for lists of Garebian's books, none seems comprehensive. So, start your compilation of his titles with his own website: https://garebian.wordpress.com/about/
5. He has since won several literary awards, but perhaps the most prestigious are The William Saroyan Medal (2013) from Armenia and the Naji Namaan Literary Honour Prize from Lebanon (2009).
6. Keith Garebian, *Blue: The Derek Jarman Poems* (Winnipeg: Signature Editions, 2008).
7. See Garebian, *against forgetting*, p. 30.
8. Note that, in his colour author photo, Garebian sports a dark-blue shirt.

9. See George Elliott Clarke, "Sighting the Giallo in Ho Che Anderson's Graphic Texts" in *Transformations of the Canadian Cultural Mosaic.* Anna Pia De Luca and Deborah Saidero, eds. (Udine, IT: Centro di Cultura Canadese, Università degli Studi di Udine, 2012), p. 63.
10. Keith Garebian, *Georgia and Alfred* (Toronto: Quattro Books, 2015).
11. Garebian, *Georgia and Alfred*, p. 20.
12. Garebian, *Georgia and Alfred*, p. 46.
13. *Das Ewig-Weibliche*, the Eternal Feminine, a phrase from Goethe's *Faust*, Garebian reports (*Georgia and Alfred*, p. 70).
14. Garebian, *Georgia and Alfred*, p. 91.
15. "Pedestrianism" is a fault that vitiates other Garebian poems. This problem afflicts works wherein he believes that he can let his subjects "speak for themselves" *via* literal quotation. (Lookit! In writing a poetry *book*, a poet has to be a poet *all the time.*)
16. Or should that be "Blue Is a Whole"?
17. Keith Garebian, *Children of Ararat* (Calgary: Frontenac House, 2010).
18. Keith Garebian, *Pain: Journeys Around My Parents* (Oakville, ON: Mosaic Press, 2000).
19. Keith Garebian, *Reservoir of Ancestors* (Oakville, ON: Mosaic Press, 2003).
20. I quote from the statement of the 2010 jury whose members selected the manuscript of "Children of Ararat" as a work that Frontenac House should publish.
21. Keith Garebian, *Poetry Is Blood* (Toronto: Guernica Editions, 2018).

Staging Six Decades of Canadian Theatre History

ROBIN BREON

Keith Garebian is a person who needs no introduction but I would like to give him one anyway. Those familiar with his work, know him as an author, poet, theatre critic and educator who, for his entire life, has been a passionate supporter of the arts in general and the art of the theatre in particular.

His reviews and articles have appeared in a wide cross-section of Canadian journals in both the popular as well as the academic press. You would have to look long and hard for a newspaper, popular journal, magazine or anthology in Canada in which Dr. Garebian has not published. His prolific and award-winning poetry has been translated and published internationally and there are many readers who know Keith Garebian as a poet first and a theatre reviewer and author of biographies second. As a book reviewer, his insightful pieces appear regularly in *Literary Review of Canada*.

Full disclosure: I know Garebian primarily as a colleague in the business of reviewing plays. I would regularly run into him on many opening nights, particularly for international plays and musicals that were receiving their Canadian premiere. On these occasions I was always eager to know his opinion.

But before I even asked the question: "Have you seen the play already?" I knew the answer. He would reply, courtly, "Oh yes, I saw it in the West End" or "I saw it when it opened on Broadway." Always kind of drawing out the word "Brooooadway," just to give it a bit more inflection and make me all the more envious that I would not be able to compare the original company with the players we would be seeing that night on stage.

That is the Keith Garebian I know, an inveterate theatre-goer who knows of what he speaks because he can make objective comparisons and judgements that are not just randomly pulled out of a hat.

When I say Garebian is a biographer, I mean to use the word in its widest sense and application. As an author, he has made a valuable contribution by writing biographies of five hallmark Broadway musicals (*Gypsy*, *My Fair Lady*, *West Side Story*, *Guys & Dolls*, and *Cabaret*) as well as his acclaimed two-volume biography of the actor, William Hutt.

The William Hutt bio was developed in two volumes published some years apart. *Masks and Faces* (Mosaic Press, 1995) was published on the occasion of Hutt's seventy-fifth birthday. It encompasses twenty-six short sketches divided into three parts: The Actor, The Director and The Man, with an assemblage of contributors who had known and worked with Hutt over the years, including Herbert Whittaker, Richard Monette, Diana Leblanc, Peter Moss, Barbara Budd, Patricia Hamilton, and James Blendick—to name a few.

Did Garebian's personal friendship with Hutt (that developed over a total period of twenty-three years) co-opt his objectivity on the subject matter? Although the author remains a fierce partisan on the life and times of William Hutt, Garebian certainly does spill the tea from time to time, which only makes his books more fun to read. This first reflection on Hutt's life and work was an attempt to, as the editor/contributor put it, "keep faith with his past, present and future as an actor." True that.

At the age of seventy-five, Hutt still had an impressive future as an actor ahead of him at the Stratford Festival and beyond, including roles such as Falstaff in The *Merry Wives of Windsor*;

James Tyrone in *Long Day's Journey Into the Night* (stage and film versions); *King Lear* (his fourth run at the role); Benjamin Hubbard in The *Little Foxes*; Prospero in *The Tempest* (1999); Henry Drummond in *Inherit the Wind*; the King of France in *All Well's That Ends Well*; another run at Prospero in 2005, and, finally, his perfectly framed performance as Charles Kingman, the aged lion of the fictional New Burbage Shakespeare Festival, in the third season of the Canadian television series, *Slings and Arrows* (2006).

If the arts world kept statistics the way the sports world does, William Hutt's lifetime achievement from 1948 - 2008 would place him right up there among the world's MVPs.

In *Slings and Arrows*, Hutt (as Kingman) is cast as King Lear, despite the fact that his age and declining health do not augur well for the production's success. He persistently intimidates everyone around him including a hard put-upon Sarah Polley who is cast as Cordelia opposite Hutt's domineering Kingman/ Lear. After years of intermittent viewing of Hutt's performance in *Slings and Arrows* (written by Mark McKinney, Susan Coyne and Bob Martin), I judge it to be a performance so poignant, finely tuned and heartfelt, that it still necessitates the aid of a handkerchief in the watching. Like Charles Kingman fighting for his life in *Slings and Arrows*, Hutt would die from cancer within twelve months after the series ended.

They say it is difficult for an author to choose one work that they extol over everything else they have ever written. A journalist once asked Joseph Heller why it was that he never wrote anything that topped his novel, *Catch-22*. He answered that he didn't know why but that no one else had either. I suspect that Keith Garebian might consider *William Hutt: Soldier Actor* to be his *magnum opus*. Regardless as to whether this is true or not, published ten years after Hutt's death, the book stands as the most comprehensive and authoritative biography of one of Canada's foremost actors and a chronicle that will not be topped by anyone, anytime soon.

William Ian DeWitt Hutt was born on May 2, 1920, the son of Edward and Caroline Hutt at Women's Hospital in Toronto. On the paternal side of his family, he was of Pennsylvania Dutch stock. In Pennsylvania that included early Dutch and German farmers and tradespeople who mainly followed the Protestant (including Mennonite and Amish) faiths. In Hutt's family, all of the male line were given the middle name, DeWitt, which literally means, "the blond one" or "the white one."

So, it should come as no surprise that young Bill Hutt's first recorded brush with performance was by way of a Christmas pageant in which he played a vendor in Bethlehem's market place. Although his parents had little interest in supporting theatre as a career, young William continued his interest in elocution and training by way of high school oratory contests and small roles in plays.

His education was abruptly interrupted by the outbreak of World War II. He joined the Canadian Armed Forces and served as a member of the army ambulance corps on the front lines of the Italian campaign. His service as a medic brought him into close encounters with injury and death on a regular basis, and his subsequent belief in the sacredness and fragility of every life never left him.

During leave times from active duty, he was able to journey to London at a time when service personnel (which also included nurses and others serving on the home front) were treated with great generosity by the arts community. Complimentary tickets for theatre, opera and the ballet were made available to soldiers in uniform and Hutt wasted no time taking in as much theatre as he could. He recalled in interviews over the years, that it was this period that made him believe that he might have what it takes to be an actor.

Hutt believed he had the ability, disposition, talent and commitment to call himself an actor—but most of all he had the opportunity. He came of age artistically during the years after the Second World War that were the real "building years" for Canadian arts and cultural institutions across the country. With public funding from federal and provincial governments in the vanguard, Canada was ready to enjoin the early cultural battles that would attempt to distinguish the country (ever so gradually) from its colonial past with Great Britain and to establish future demarcations from the domineering cultural presence of its neighbour to the south.

These early years of the Canadian theatre movement are described with great flavour and detail by Garebian in the early chapters of the book. In the summer of 1948, still in Hutt's pre-Stratford life as an actor, we find him working in Bracebridge, Ontario, with a newly formed group called the Mark Shawn Players. At the end of the season, the company went belly up financially and Hutt found himself stranded in Bracebridge, unemployed.

Unable to find work in the theatre, he took a job as a bricklayer to see himself through the winter months financially. He would later remark: "It was a time in life when one was just pressing on with a faint glow of hope on one's face, looking toward a very insecure future. Nonetheless, it was exciting, simply because we never knew how far it was going to carry us all."

Garebian's subtext of Hutt's life as a homosexual in Toronto's surreptitious gay subculture, when gays were deep in the closet, is a welcome addition to "queering the history" projects that helps the reader to understand the strict moral codes and ever vigilant police threats always on the lookout for "indecent" behaviour that oppressed gay lifestyles during this period and long afterwards. As a man who discovered his gay identity later in life, Garebian is able to sensitively explore the difficulties Hutt experienced in coming out to family and close friends, not all of whom were sympathetic.

It was during these early years of touring across Canada and the U.S. with the Canadian Players and also working with the Ottawa based Canadian Repertory Theatre, that Hutt came to learn about the theatre profession in both countries. Early on in his career, he decided it was in Canada that he wanted to live and work.

On July 13, 1953, The Stratford Shakespearean Festival of Canada (its formally incorporated name at the time) went from a gleam in the eye of a local Stratford journalist named Tom Patterson, to a sword in the hand of Alec Guinness playing the leading role in *Richard the Third*, directed by Tyrone Guthrie. Seventy years on, the Stratford Festival has become the Olympus of repertory theatre in North America.

With no real formal training in the theatre and certainly little experience with Shakespeare, Hutt found himself cast in the inaugural Stratford company in the small roles of James Blunt / Robert Brakenbury in *Richard III* and Minister of State in *All's Well That Ends Well.* The experience gained during those first seasons at Stratford would be tantamount to an undergraduate B.A. in dramatic art from any post-graduate educational institution today.

With "professor" Guthrie at the helm of this first graduating class, Hutt was able to observe seasoned professionals and learn from the very best. From the beginning, Guthrie believed that the Canadian theatre should be uniquely that – Canadian. "I think the Canadians can speak English clearer and better to the English-speaking world and be readily understood than even our English actors," he observed early in his tenure at Stratford.

Over the years, Hutt's roles increased in size as Stratford's reputation continued to grow as a "destination point" (as the travel industry calls it) for classical theatre in North America. Garebian's portrayal of these early years, especially the Guthrie period, gives the reader an idea of the real commitment it takes to grow a cultural institution, as well as a behind the scenes look at the productions that sometimes went awry. His description of Guthrie's production of Christopher Marlowe's play, *Tamburlaine the Great,* with its huge cast of 76 actors that played the Royal Alexandra Theatre before proceeding on to a Broadway run is not to be missed. It makes *The Play That Goes Wrong* look not all that bad in comparison.

This is all part of the history, myth and legend of what is today called (more simply than its originally incorporated title) The Stratford Festival. Through it all, William Hutt found a place to grow artistically, with a job that afforded some financial security (in an industry that is infamous for its precarity) and, quite literally, a home of his own only a short walk from the theaters in which he labored so long and so successfully.

Speaking of Hutt's style and idiosyncrasies as an actor, Garebian includes this bit of insight from Christopher Plummer: "It is impossible to underplay William Hutt, and this makes him a dangerous fellow to act with on stage." I can relate to this observation with one of my own from a production of *All's Well That Ends Well* at Stratford during the 2002 season.

With a bit of honest self-deprecation on my part, I admit to two things as one who has written many play reviews over the years: I am by no means a Shakespearean scholar and I never like to read or reread a script before I see a production. I like to see the play unfold in front of me, just like every other member of the audience. Some Shakespeare plays are more familiar to me than others; *All's Well That Ends Well* is one that I was a bit fuzzy on plot details.

It is with this in mind, that I attended the 2002 production of *AWTEW* that introduces the King of France in the second scene of the first act. The King (played by Hutt) is already seated centre-stage on his throne as the lights come up. The King greets members of the court and speaks about some business between the Florentines and the Senoys. As he drones on, I found myself leaning in—not only a bit bored by Hutt's performance but also increasingly concerned. His words were garbled, in a low, almost inaudible register that led me to wonder if the man might be ill. Of course, at the end of the scene, it is quite apparent to all that the King, who cannot rise from his throne without assistance, is indeed ill, almost on his deathbed in fact. End of Act I, scene 2. My eyes were riveted on the King for the entire scene. Damn, that guy's good!

William Hutt: Soldier Actor

ROBIN BREON

The title of this biography (Guernica Editions, 2017) was adapted from Hutt's epitaph. It is at once literal and figurative in meaning. Hutt was a soldier who was awarded a medal for bravery in battle as well as a combatant in the early culture wars that slowly began to carve out our uniquely modern Canadian identity in both Anglophone and Francophone worlds.

I sometimes wonder what William Hutt would think of the Stratford Festival today, over a decade after his passing. The recognition that the Festival is no longer the sole privilege of "the white ones" is now a matter of official record and that, to my mind, is a good thing.

The Festival has gone so far as to hire a director for Equity, Diversity and Inclusion, one of the most ubiquitous job postings in the arts and cultural sector to be seen over the past few years in North America after the events of the past decade identified by grass roots movements such as "We See You White (North) American Theatre" and other allies who focused on institutional racism as a barrier for racialized minorities in arts organizations across the continent. Hutt might grumble a bit, but I would like to think his generosity of spirit would embrace the changes.

In a passionate summation of Hutt's life as an actor, Garebian proclaims: "He never imitated any other actor in any major role; his Pandarus was a genuine original that has never been matched ; his Titus owed nothing to Olivier; his James Tyrone was never in the shadow of Frederic March; his Tartuffe was Planchon-free; his Falstaff, like his Feste, was his and his alone; and his Lady Bracknell was the first great transvestite acting of the part, high camp but peerless in its sense of comedy and its audience."

In *William Hutt: Soldier Actor*, Keith Garebian has not only provided a valuable biography of a great actor but an invaluable history of the Canadian theatre from the post WW2 years onward. Prodigious research leg-work for over two decades has produced a collection of first-person interviews, referenced primary documents of the period and personal observations and commentary that makes the book come alive as living history. Anecdotal comments from a cornucopia of theatre luminaries (I could name drop here but the list is far too long) and early pioneers of the Canadian theatre movement only add flavor and spice to this remarkable serving of our cultural heritage.

William Hutt was a soldier, an actor and a bricklayer, who steadfastly dedicated himself to laying down the foundations of this country's professional theatre at a time when the going was rough and the political will was only fledgling at best. Today, our artists have just survived another rough time, a war against nature in the form of a pandemic that no one could have imagined would take such a ferocious toll on our profession.

But the artists and the arts that they serve continue on in spite of reactionary politicians who once again are seeing the arts as a soft target at which to take (sometimes literal) pot shots while increasing military spending over arts funding and making fighter jets and submarines priorities over peace-making and a green economy. In the midst of it all, the spirits of the early soldiers and pioneers like William Hutt, press on with a resolve that leaves no doubt the creative arts in Canada must and will survive.

William Hutt: Soldier Actor

DAVID BATEMAN

Biographer, poet, and theatre scholar Keith Garebian's 542-page biography of William Hutt (Guernica Editions, 2017) may seem daunting at first glance, but very quickly one is drawn into an almost novel-like epic adventure that manages to take the life of a single iconic Canadian actor and mould it into a seamless narrative that never fails to enlighten, amuse, and instill admiration for one of the most compelling performing arts careers of the 20th century. And if that's not enough, other men and women acclaimed in both film and theatre cross the boards of Garebian's mammoth achievement, making his contribution both personal and inclusive as it adds to the rich, often unsung history of Canada's theatrical history, and the ways in which it has frequently crossed paths with international glory.

Christopher Plummer, Martha Henry, Brian Bedford, Maggie Smith, Noel Coward, Sybil Thorndike, and William Shatner lounge among the ranks of star powered creatures whose fame brushed lightly—at times even brashly—against Hutt's diverse and lavish career. During a meeting regarding Hutt's part in *Waiting in the Wings* (Broadway, 1960) Noel Coward told him, "You don't have to sing much, darling ... Maybe one little patter song. But there will be several good scenes for you." (125) A short paragraph later, the anecdote is elaborated upon when Hutt's own words evoke a detailed sense of what it was like to be directed by Coward, a tactful master:

"It's Noel's gift to make you feel as if what you're doing is right and important. In making a correction, he will say, 'Nothing to worry about, dear, but could you possibly do it a bit differently.'

Now that's tact." This brief yet concise segment also manages to include the fact that Hutt discovered, in an early rehearsal, that one of his two scenes had been changed to a musical number. Ever the tactful manipulator, Coward's satiric sense, both onstage and off, according to Hutt, was always "impeccable."

The book is filled with similar personal anecdotes that convey a sense of a detailed series of relationships and chronologies that make up a rich and varied life. Garebian also manages that delicate task of constructing a sense of Hutt's sexual and gender identities without the explicit nature some readers might crave. His companions/lovers, what have you, subtly grace the pages with an elegant sense of the writer's respect for privacy, yet titillate simultaneously through the use of photographs, a sense of intermittent conflict, up close and faintly personal anecdotes, and a heartfelt writing style that shows the author's respect for his subject. Effeminacy in particular becomes something, onstage and off, that Garebian develops in a simultaneously complex yet subtly engaging manner:

> Hutt's next role followed in 1963 when he accepted an invitation to play Pandarus in ringlets and heavy jewels in *Troilus and Cressida.* Hutt sensed all through rehearsals that Michael Langham wanted him to think like a woman for the part of the go-between between the two title lovers. At first, he did not take to Langham's direction, feeling "not quite prepared to reveal to the theatre-going public that there was a strong streak of femininity" in him. Langham recognized the stumbling block and was determined to remove it. The release came after an ivory flywhisk was put in Hutt's hand, because the prop suddenly became a focus for gesture and, behind this, for mental character. Hutt described how the process developed: "I began to think like a woman, and the final note was literally just before I went on the opening night. I suddenly took a deep breath and said, 'My God, I've got

> tits!' I went out there thinking I had a huge pair of tits, and all the things Michael had been telling me fell into place. He wanted effeminacy but not necessarily homosexuality. If the audience said, 'Oh, he's a wonderful old "queer,"' then that was a decision they should make. In other words, he didn't say, 'I want you to play this like some mad "queer" from Third Avenue.' No. He realized that it was too tight an image, too pedestrian and far too easy.

Hutt's mixed persona, in a familial role molded by birth, society and "nature" appears to be a dance between traditional, complex notions of gender and the ways in which he may have chosen to portray these traits in his personal life, his family life, and the many roles he took onto the stage. As the son of a religious man and a doting mother, with the added ingredient of an at times conflicted relationship with his brother, readers may glean engaging sex/gender details and cultural innuendoes throughout Garebian's research and anecdotal analysis. The actor/soldier's appearance in WW2 is deftly handled and reveals a fine balance between time spent both fighting and 'acting' for his country. There is an especially fascinating correlation between Hutt's bravery during a dangerous episode in Italy, and the ways in which he was able to bring extreme bravery, strength and character to the roles he would encounter when he returned to Canada and began to pursue an acting career. A colleague once observed the soldier actor mentality that led Hutt through his many roles in life and gave him a special cadence, intuition, and rhythm that frequently worked well onstage, opting for a knowing patience rather than a frustrated and cumbersome pose:

> There was never frustration. If he wasn't sure of something, he would ask a question, but there was never a whole lot of conversation about something. You could see that he had done a

> lot of thinking, and if he had a question, he would hash it out in rehearsal. If he wasn't comfortable with a moment, he didn't need to sit and chat about it. He really was a man of action. He was a soldier that way. I remember the very opening when he came in from the heath in the play. He'd come to this man's sumptuous house. He'd walk in, but he didn't want to walk across the rug for fear he would leave marks on it, so he did this very simple walk around the contours of the rug, and it was hilarious. He was playful, and yet he was masterful at knowing what would work and what wouldn't with an audience. It just seemed to be organic—a second sense.

Elaborating on Hutt's rehearsal method, Hughes noted that he was very precise in what he did but would never use his full power either in rehearsals or in previews:

> Unlike some actors who come out of the chute and just blow it out, he was the other way. You could see him clocking when the audience responded. He was using the previews to figure out where he was going, and each night, he added another 15%, as he became more and more assured of where he was going, how he was going to use his audience, and how he was going to engage with the actors on stage with this new dance partner—the audience. So, by the opening, he was cooking, he was just flying and right where he needed to be. Bill was never more or any less than he needed to be. It was a great lesson.

Garebian, however, is not all smiles and acclaim in his in-depth reading of Hutt's varied career. Late in the book, at the beginning of his epilogue, he candidly admits to being the discerning critic who does not allow his status as a great admirer of Hutt's to become an entirely one-sided tome of fandom and unwarranted praise:

> When I approached him in 1984 to write his biography, I was honest about my own reservations. I had certainly admired him in most of his roles, but I did not like his Claudius for John Neville or his first attempt at the King of France in *All's Well That Ends Well*, and I had criticisms of his Vanya for Robin Phillips and his first Falstaff in *The Merry Wives of Windsor*. When inspiration or taste or daring failed him, he was grossly hammy or merely dull. I had heard of his ego, and I decided to test his limits by telling him at the outset that I considered Sir Laurence Olivier to be the greatest actor I had ever seen and the only theatre idol, apart from Shakespeare, that I revered. He eyed me coldly at first, probably amazed at my impertinent audacity. I could have become a live sacrifice at 4 Waterloo North, but he kept his temper well under control. I believe he even began to respect me a little for my honesty and nerve, though he must have winced privately at my calculated tactlessness. It was essential, however, to serve him advance notice that I would not be writing hagiography. And he surprised me, in turn, by his outward placidity.

Ultimately the book becomes a lightly sparring relationship between biographer and subject, whereby the individuals collaborate, over a span of many years, on detailed encounters that achieve a fine and delicate balance between biography, personal narrative, and astute critique:

> [At the] Chalmers Awards at the St. Lawrence Centre on January 30, 1989, at which he was to receive the Toronto Drama Bench Award ... Looking elegant and relaxed, Hutt made a witty acceptance speech, thanking Sylvia Shawn for giving him his first professional job, Amelia Hall for her generosity, Tony Guthrie for his love, Langham for his style, Gascon for his energy and warmth, John Hirsch for his deficit, and Robin Phillips, above all, for setting a new direction for his career. He also thanked

the critical fraternity for having tried to keep him humble over all these years—"which according to the recent book by Keith Garebian is no easy task."

Garebian has written about Hutt's life before and comes back to the front, in his latest venture, with an immense and valuable contribution to Canadian theatre history, as well as an homage to a kind of Canadian career that we can all learn patience, admiration, and respect from as we continue to muddle through the cumbersome performance of identity that being Canadian, both onstage and off, entails.

The final pages, nearing Hutt's death in 2007, incorporate remarkably beautiful and moving portraits of an icon in one of his final courageous and generous performances:

> Journalist Sandra Martin of *The Globe and Mail* visited him on a clear, sunny day in early June, ostensibly to fact check things about his life story, and Hutt, attached to a portable oxygen machine, was unable to rise from his wing chair beside a window to receive her. His face a waxy pallor and dressed in "a loose, brown-patterned shirt over casual trousers, and with terribly swollen ankles showing above a pair of moccasins," he began the interview by asking: "Have you ever interviewed anyone who's actually dying?" (Martin June 28, 2007) The question took her by surprise, as did his subsequent conversation of almost ninety minutes, during which, though racked by coughs, he talked frankly about his parents, the war, and his introduction to death before he had a chance to know much about life. He indicated three major stages in his life: adolescence, "when things happen to your body and your mind"; your twenties, when "your parents become your friends rather than authority figures"; and death, the stage he was entering with questions of what it would be like. He was modest about his own capacities as an actor: "I will leave

> the word 'great' to history, but I do know that in some kind of way, my career as an actor has paralleled the growth of theatre in this country." He had always been pragmatic, and he explained that his decision to stay home rather than to chase fame and fortune in London and New York came from an "an arrogant pride" in Canada. "I had no intention of leaving this country until I was invited. I wasn't going to beg." He acknowledged the generous friendship and support of Richard Monette: "He has prolonged my life and my career."

In *William Hutt: Soldier Actor* Keith Garebian has further prolonged the career of a man and a nationality through exhaustive research, personal admiration, astute critique, and a commitment to chronicling detailed, entertaining, and engaging accounts of Canadian theatre history and all of its complex creatures.

against forgetting

Memory Through a Refracted Postcolonial Gaze: A Review

DAVID BATEMAN

Keith Garebian's *against forgetting* (Frontenac House, 2019) develops the poet's ongoing passion for memory. Ethnicity, education, and the presence of paternal lineage continue the poet's exploration of family history and evoke a strong and engaging sense of intergenerational discourse. Maternal images arise throughout, giving the collection a powerful, conflicted, yet loving sense of intersecting cultural/familial influences that have shaped the writer's life and practice.

"Mimicry," a pivotal poem, balances a powerful citational tone by inserting an instructional and poetic meditation. The concept of mimicking indirectly references Homi Bhabha's work on hybridity, whereby individuals living within colonized societies take on the culture of the colonizers. As a poet/theatre arts journalist/actor, Garebian adeptly navigates this balancing act in his life and in his work. His heritage contributes to an exquisitely refracted and deconstructionist way of perceiving past, present, and future. "Mimicry" straddles all of these time periods, creating a reflective space for the reader to consider the pages and the words that have come before:

> I was never in love with the mud tablets
> of Indian provinces, manacled mantras,
> saffron Benares, the inner ears of shells ...
> Their styles were beyond my mimicry.

This pointed list, culled from the memory of the poet's life as a queer artist born to an Armenian father and an Anglo-Indian mother, constructs a configurative identity that reveals many aspects of a refracted postcolonial gaze. "Mimicry" quickly moves, as do many of the poems in *against forgetting,* into another list of memories originating within particular literary and cultural experiences that Garebian encountered at a very early age:

> in school, imitation was imperative
> in writing. We copied or echoed,
> in elegant murmurs, fastidious facsimiles,
> morphing into literary mimics ...
> some virtue in our practice:
> mimicry showed variety
> in being adept.

This personal take on postcolonialism renders colonialist intrusion a challenge that the subject utilizes to his advantage. The echoes and murmurs of Garebian's self-identified virtue lend an essential conflict and rhythmic power to a decidedly racialized gaze—a gaze inflected here and there with subtle gestures toward the queerness lying at the homosocial heart of the writer's tone and subject matter: "School dances, chastely homosocial, / chaperoned by teachers, priests, / and asexual parents." ("Jesuits, Shri, and Sex")

Nearing the end of the collection this queerness gently surfaces again in "Second Country" as eloquently nonchalant rhythms are cited from Frank O'Hara's poem "A True Account of Talking to the Sun at Fire Island": "Don't worry about your lineage / poetic or natural. / The sun shines on." Garebian's poems always worry, in elegant, explorative and powerful ways, about lineage—cultural and literary. He crafts memory through rich tapestries of identity in order to both rage against and pay homage to a past that shapes a future. This gentle rage against forgetting resists the potential loss of all that has gone into the construction of a particular poetic voice. All the world, a varied post-colonial stage, as Shakespeare—Garebian's lowercase "god" ("We Are Unalike, This Land That Houses Me")—rules. The iconic bard frequently guides Garebian's literary trajectories as spaces for high drama marked by sharp sighted poetic reflection.

against forgetting moves across borders from India to England, and ultimately Canada, finding theatrical solace and colonial grandeur in the mouths of colonized schoolchildren, actors (e.g. Sir Laurence Olivier), and queer poets, ultimately resting in the final line of a stunning collection by an artfully insightful colonized soul: "The past is here." ("Self-portrait in A New World")

Finger to Finger

Something Like Intimacy: A Review

DAVID BATEMAN

Keith Garebian's collections of deeply personal poetry range from his 2018 collection *Poetry Is Blood* (Guernica Editions) depicting the brutal realities of the Armenian genocide, to his 2022 exploration of local geography (*in the bowl of my eye*, Mawenzi House) as counterpoint to the personal landscapes of people and places he encounters with diverse purviews of character and locale—"in my suburban Mississauga world." *Finger to Finger* (Frontenac House, 2022) is his most intimate collection to date. The work combines intimacy with objectivity, weaving a Brechtian sense of epic narrative—gesturing toward a vast global and political environment—with a queer writer's observations of the world at large. Moving deeply into poignancy and self-interrogation as the poet tackles the death of an ex-wife (the mother of his only child) with an honesty that both endears and alienates in a sometimes raw, frequently enlightening manner.

Beginning with an engagement marked by a band of gold "with a small defect" metonymically leading to an unexpected outcome ("We never predicted the dark / coldness, love emptied, / sapphire of ash"), the poet journeys toward a mixed conception of love and grief as childbirth inspires joy, becoming complex self-reflection:

> My boy, you were needed
> desperately, for your mother
> and I had gone sour ...

you became
my loving, dark-haired son,
with something like intimacy
between us.

Self-reflection leaps into more intense moments with a prolonged section devoted to wife, mother, child. The narrative skillfully deploys seamless storytelling and standalone poems as sexual diversity unfolds, revealing the shadowed alienation inscribed on the queer body:

trapped in a ship in a bottle
drifting on sea-foam,
at the mercy of the fickle
tides. We are, each of us,
the ocean in a beached shell,
yearning for the song of ourselves ...

Queerness stands in for a kind of epic alternative identity that reflects the movement from specific sexuality to a romantic blur—lifetimes of loving (carnally and emotionally) both men and women. Faint, seductive eroticism surfaces in beautifully wrought lines that emphasize metaphor and manliness in a single image:

young soldiers with guns
nestling low near their groins
under camouflage uniforms.
As we drift by, one locks eyes
with me, under a mournful banyan.

The banyan as hovering body, desirous and overhanging in its shadowed presence.

Halfway through, the poet makes a complex apology in perhaps the most honest and self-interrogating moment, exclaiming, in light of the loaded question, "Have you ever been intimate with another man?"—"I wish I had given a better answer." Then the honesty of resisted sharing follows: "I wanted to tell her / my feelings for men. / I wanted to open/ the thick curtains, / let the starlight in," moving with a painful yet gorgeous effortlessness toward "Just arms around my neck, / lips brushing mine, / a body shimmering / in apical noonday mirage. / Gender neutral."

Apex—life moments—as self-realization, assuring no neutrality in this collection as *Finger to Finger* exemplifies life transitions shrouded in social dysphoria framed strenuously by complex forms of sensual and emotional desire.

in the bowl of my eye & Finger to Finger

A Review

JOHN OUGHTON

Keith Garebian is well known both for his poetry and his literary and drama criticism. Some veteran poets find a modus operandi that includes certain themes or settings and ways to write about them that becomes a comfortable rut. There may be some wonderful poems in their later work, but their approach is no surprise. Garebian is not that kind of poet. I will approach his latest two books, *in the bowl of my eye* (Mawenzi House, 2022) and *Finger to Finger* (Frontenac House, 2022) in the order in which I read them.

As the author's note states, "*in the bowl of my eye* is a radical departure from my previous poetic themes and aesthetic practices." The heart of this book is place, specifically the Lakeshore area of Etobicoke and Mississauga. But rather than extolling the beauties of the lake or autumn leaves, Garebian declares, "I have sought to refuse familiar tropes of nature poetry." Most of the poems concern neighbours and community members or his own life there. As one might expect from a writer so adept at criticism, there is little sentimentality here. Even though quotations from Walt Whitman introduce sections of the book, Garebian does not follow Whitman in embracing all humankind, seeking the common spirit in himself and others. I don't mean that the voice here lacks compassion, passion or love, but that his sharp perception isolates each subject almost clinically. In this book, he is more the flâneur, noting those he passes without necessarily engaging with them. Hence the title—he's inspired by what lingers in the bowl of his eye.

There's an echo of Yeats's self-selected epitaph here: "Cast a cold eye, on life, on death. Horseman, pass by." Speaking of other writers, the author works their lines into his own in an intriguing way. Rather than using them just as an epigraph at the kick-off, they're woven into the poems, as if the resonance suddenly occurred to him. He incorporates quotations from Wendell Berry, Nietzsche, Susan Glickman, Bruce Meyer, and others, shifting the poems from an inner monologue to a conversation with the larger literary world.

These poems are set in suburbia, a liminal space between the grittier big cities and the open fields and farms. As the speaker says in "Suburban Purgatory":

> suburbia being ex-urban
> pedestrian, minds as finely clipped
> as lawns luxuriating in weed-killer.

Suburbia is not traditionally a fertile place for inspiring poems. Yet Garebian, without romanticizing his locale, views it as a space as uncertain as Hong Kong, with its protests and repression, or as the US mired in toxic politics, interweaving lines from the Irish poet Eavan Boland in "Prologue":

> And I live in suburbia,
> no paradise or Sahara.
> Suburbia, I know too well
> "the kitchen bulbs
> which blister your dark"

Some poems are quiet, carefully pared observations. Others surprise with a sudden punch—like "You Who Knew the Name of Every Plant," about his relationship with a gardener (his second wife), which concludes, "We smell of mortality." Formally, all are free verse and unrhymed, but there is considerable variation in line breaks, overall length, and use of stanzas. This echoes the fact that each poem addresses a different subject or a distinct way of experiencing the world.

Finger to Finger, despite its different themes, has some commonalities with *in the bowl of my eye.* One is the cosmopolitan, globe-trotting sophistication of a writer born in India to an Armenian father and Anglo-Indian mother, who then moved with them to Canada, and has travelled extensively himself. Another is Garebian's honesty, calling things as he sees them. He strips bare his own confusions and illuminations without overly lyrical imagery or evasions. This is an intriguing approach for a poet who also writes, "the dream was the heart / lying to itself the way poetry sometimes does."

Finger to Finger focuses on more personal issues, particularly relationships, marriages, the death of parents, raising a child, and exploring one's sexuality. The title, which at first recalled for me Michelangelo's famous image of God creating Adam, is drawn from a poem about Garebian's last contact with a dying ex-wife. Garebian reveals that he has had relationships with both men and women. He writes about these with both directness and tenderness, noting that caring for another can survive even a break-up. He does not spare his own errors and hesitations during the hard work of loving others. As he puts it in "Mind Swallows Itself":

> as I write,
> hoping to forgive myself
> for so often prizing books above
> humans

I found the final poem in this collection the most moving. Inspired by a throat cancer diagnosis, in "Lost in Old Age," the poet confronts the meaning of life and death in indelible lines:

> we're no longer part
> of the universe's phantom design,
> we have been writing
> ourselves on sand, on water

He ends with a couplet that neatly encapsulates the paradox in understanding that we will end, at least in our current and mortal forms: "our exhausted wake, as we sleep to rouse the infinite." Such lines make this reader hope that these two collections are not Garebian's final words in poetic form.

Rereading *in the bowl of my eye*

DOROTHY SJÖHOLM

I rarely reread poetry books in their entirety, opting instead to dip into them here and there, savouring those poems that, to quote Robert Frost, find a way of "taking life by the throat." Yet my dog-eared copy of Keith Garebian's *in the bowl of my eye* (Mawenzi House, 2022) with its underlinings and marginalia bears witness to many rereadings from cover to cover. What is it that continues to draw me back to this work focused on vulnerable people in Mississauga on the edge of Lake Ontario and a struggling natural world?

When I first encountered *in the bowl of my eye* it was in manuscript form, and I found myself enthralled by the indefinable magic of its words in spite of the ordinariness of the setting. The poems were both carefully crafted and layered, offering fresh insights with each rereading. And, though written by an immigrant with an Armenian-Anglo-Indian background, they somehow seemed utterly Canadian to me—a response which, like all generalizations, I realize is inherently flawed, but which I choose to explore here simply because it was my initial, and somewhat surprising, gut reaction.

Given the fact that school curricula focused on British and American poets when I was young, it may be a contrarian nature that has led me to consistently seek out good Canadian poetry in my adult life. Regardless of cause, that is a tendency with me, and the book *in the bowl of my eye* is clearly the work of a poet who has mastered his craft and has a clarity and depth of vision that renders his poems both Canadian and thematically universal, thus holding a double appeal.

Of course, people's concepts of what constitutes "Canadian" literature vary, and those of us who studied the anthologies of Edmund Wilson along with literary theories expounded in Northrop Frye's *The Bush Garden* and Margaret Atwood's *Survival* may view things differently from younger generations. Writing topics, concepts, and styles evolve. But as recently as 2021 novelist Stephen Marche wrote "So much Canadian art boils down to landscape," (*National Geographic* 8.20.2021). This seems to me to be inherently true, especially if one includes the effect landscape has on its inhabitants, the inhabitants' attitude toward the natural world, and the interior landscape created by this interaction.

Would the poet himself consider this book to be typically Canadian? Perhaps not. Each section, after all, begins with a quotation from Walt Whitman's *Song of Myself,* and the poem "Prologue" opens with references to Barcelona and Hong Kong. But the focus of "Prologue" narrows down to "measured solitude / in a site worn by unmarked echoes," and the initial Author's Note, prepares us for a series of poems that are "a radical departure from [Garebian's] previous poetic themes and aesthetic practices" (vii). Here we encounter a new focus on and connection with the natural world, "a lake which organizes itself/as assorted birds dip and float / stones with natural texts," and a community of immigrants and others who seem to struggle with feelings of alienation—"humans unwinding themselves" in a Canadian setting.

The world of these poems is Suburbia, far removed from what one might consider typical or traditional Canadian nature poems such as Lampman's "Temagami" or Campbell's "Snow." Garebian sees his natural surroundings realistically as they currently exist in Mississauga. Yet he also imagines them as they once were, as they have evolved. He portrays a land which, though younger than his birthplace, "tells the same truth:/land births us." In "Prologue to a New World," he tells us:

> Suburbia lures my eyes to open wide
> to the savage and the singular
> as my mind shapes thoughts
> sharp as pine needles, cool
> as clear lake water.

The sensory appeal of these lines, and the sibilance of "Suburbia ... savage and ... singular," strengthen the metaphoric allusion to natural objects with quite disparate attributes—the sharpness of needles, the coolness of water—images which may remind any student of CanLit of the works of early Canadian poets, and even of our visual artists such as Tom Thomson and Emily Carr. In my case, these images certainly came to mind. Yet I am also aware of the differences. Though Garebian has a keen and compassionate eye, he does not romanticize or attempt to infuse nature with a sense of spirituality as many early Canadian poets did. This nature exists in its creatures, objects, plants, and in a force that is "life itself—anomalous / absurd, austere, ample." ("Nature Poem")

The title "Nature Poem," and the fact that it follows "Prologue to a New World," may even suggest an ironic playfulness—an immigrant having fun with the concept of traditional Canadian poetry. Here we see a poet in transition. A man who previously "did not wish to waste [him]self / staring at the moon" or other aspects of nature has now discovered a new way to appreciate the natural world around him. This may be a "Nature Poem," but it is not about Canada's near or far north—no sled dogs, no threatening forests, no Pre-Cambrian Shield, "no noble savage"—just the natural world as it coexists with the residents of Mississauga, a world that includes "a small turtle struggling out of a furrow" ("Turtle") and a dead man floating in Lake Ontario ("Body in Lake").

This natural world leads the poet to contemplate life in general. As he watches nature, "Time ticks away / in terse wisdoms we struggle to fix" ("Poem in Late Spring"), and an observation of "Queen Anne's Lace" causes him to comment, "Not the last time for love and poison / in the same encounter." Thus, we see a poet who studies nature with the same keen eye he uses to observe humanity. Both seem to function as his classroom. In Garebian's nature poems I see similarities especially to the writings of Canadian poets of the late 20th century, reminding me, for example, of some of the works of Al Purdy. This may not be Roblin Lake or "The Country North of Belleville," but in his poems Garebian offers the same attention to detail as Purdy did in illuminating that part of Ontario, and both poets use the natural world (past and present) as a jumping-off point from which to explore the relationship between people and the land they inhabit.

In the Author's Note at the beginning of the book, Garebian writes, "In this collection I interrogate myself in my suburban Mississauga world," and goes on to say, "because much of what I write arises from the depth of intimate experience, a reader reads *the work inside me*." This is true even in the middle section of the book, which focuses on the "Lake/Road/Park", and true, perhaps, of all good poetry. It calls to mind Purdy's lines: "the thing was really inside / themselves all the time / ... / is it possible for a man / to explore himself?" ("The Northwest Passage")

Atwood comments in *Survival* on a Canadian tendency to tell animal stories from the point of view of the animal, especially if it is being hunted (pp.74 & 76) and Northrop Frye claims in *The Bush Garden* that "there is a recognizable

Canadian accent in the more highly organized speech of its poetry" (p 133). Are these qualities still characteristic of Canadian writing? Perhaps not so much in the 2020's as the internet and intersectionality hold sway. Like the land around us, our poetry evolves. But they are part of a Canadian tradition in a general and evolving sense, and clearly present in Garebian's work.

In her argument, Atwood quotes Newlove's "in any hunt I'm with the quarry," and I would like to expand Atwood's observations about animals to anyone who is victimized or the underdog in society. In this sense one may still see this identification with the quarry in younger poets. We see it, for instance, in Katherena Vermette's (*North End Love Songs*) where she identifies with disadvantaged people as well as less fortunate parts of her natural environment: "the wildflowers / [that] she feels sorry for" (p.57) in their struggle against their conquerors—both human and chemical. And I personally see this attitude in poetry books I randomly pull from my own bookshelves (Austin Clarke's *Where the Sun Shines Best, Best Canadian Poetry 2023*, Gary Geddes' *What Does a House Want,* Anne Carson's *Glass, Irony & God*)—as well as in Garebian's *in the bowl of my eye* where Evie,

> ... forever wed
> to a laminated spouse ...
>
> ... was a thin wraith
> the late night she appeared at my door,
> agitation rippling quietly
> as she asked if I had cigarettes to spare.

Throughout the series of "Suburban Portraits" that comprise the initial section of this book, the narrator empathizes with the people he portrays and seemingly asks us, his readers, to empathize likewise, or to attempt, at least, to understand their confusion, their sense of loss, their feelings of alienation arising from differences in culture (the Chinese widow in "Monday Watcher"), religion (the woman with "head bowed by the Koran" in "Mumtaz"), sexual orientation (the "Cruising gays disappearing into bushes" in "Evie"), poverty ("Old mind-blasted Lear's / throne is a ramshackle Chevy" in "Habitat"), or age ("The Old Lovers"). We find no characters here with an overweening pride in conquest, just people struggling with the difficulties of life, an empathetic watcher commenting on those struggles, and, perhaps surprisingly, an underlying sense of hope.

After first reading this manuscript, I commented that the empathetic and astute voice of the observer in these poems called to mind the "whacher" in Anne Carson's "The Glass Essay." The poems themselves, though quite different from Carson's in terms of topics and style, also share a craftsmanship and richness of allusion with Carson's work which are bound to appeal to a lover of literature. Garebian's references include direct quotations from Whitman and range from the naming of characters like Lear to the "trained trickster eyes / on Anishinaabe land" of Coyote in the parking lot ("No Frills Coyote"), a phrase alluding to colonization and reminding us that the past continues to inhabit the present even in a setting that may appear soulless. The poems are also marked by less direct allusions, for instance, the way "The Old Lovers" are described as "tilting towards some place in darkness," a phrase in which that single word "tilting" suggests a duality of meaning, reminding us of windmills as well as people who simply lean toward the dark.

While old men may be tilting at windmills or leaning toward darkness, North America seems to be "caught / in mass hypnosis by a tweeting / fraud" ("Prologue"), and an "Old Lady in Rocking Chair" is "wondering / when it will end, this slow rocking." Yet there is, throughout this book, an admiration for the human spirit and a sense of unity among humans and between humans and the natural world. The characters portrayed face conflict, a sense of alienation, loss, and dilemma. The past has shaped them, and persists, but a return to the past is not presented as an option. They must discover the best way to move forward together. "I dream unity," the speaker says. This is the "matrix / of everyday life. / One season tied to another, / like words of a poem, / fold upon fold, fond / fonts of time and its shadows." ("in the bowl of my eye")

I began with reference to the fact that I have been drawn to reread this book many times. And now I am aware that I have failed to satisfactorily explain its appeal because I have failed to adequately comment on style. Garebian is a poet who pays close attention to diction and line endings. And he uses sound and sense the way Pope suggested they should be used—as echoes, one of the other. The incantatory quality of many of the poems, including the final stanza of the final poem, serves to enchant. And the thoughtful and effective organizational structure of the book itself results in an ease of approach for all, regardless of educational or cultural background. On their own, these qualities would simply reflect knowledge of craft rather than the spark that creates an outstanding poem, the quality that merges the primal appeal of music with the insight of a keen mind. But this book offers that primal appeal as well. "I dream unity," the poet says. And these poems offer that dream for the reader to explore.

Pieces of My Self: Fragments of an Autobiography

LAURENCE HUTCHMAN

Keith Garebian's appropriately entitled memoir *Pieces of My Self: Fragments of an Autobiography* gives a candid account of the writer's life. Through these excellent pages of writing, we learn about Garebian's cultural identity of being Armenian, Anglo-Indian and, finally, Canadian, as well as his various interests in history, theatre, and poetry. The writing contains fragments, which do not tell the whole story, but by the end, they form a certain kind of wholeness.

So, why do we read memoirs of writers? They provide us with a sense of the writer's place in time, an account of significant events, the influence of other people, and the aesthetics of their literary work.

Keith Garebian begins his autobiography with a description of two important events. One is a commentary on the Armenian genocide, and the other is an account of his father's death. One could wonder why he begins his narrative that way. It's because modern Armenian history and that of his father are inextricably woven together. Garebian writes that the personal relationship between him and his father proved to be a difficult one because there was a kind of competition between them. At a young age, he reacted against his father's wishes and refused to take Armenian language classes. "I felt a secret pleasure in disappointing him by deliberately failing at Advanced Physics and Chemistry." He wrote that the silence between them increased.

Garebian never studied the Armenian language but felt "the mysterious bond between me and Armenians." His poems talk about the traumatic suffering of the people in the books *Pain: Journey Around My Parents* and *Children of Ararat.* Travelling to Armenia to attend the Fifth Conference of Writers of Armenian Origin was a life-altering experience when his name was called to receive the William Saroyan medal for his work on the Armenian Diaspora. Garebian was the first Canadian to receive this honour.

While in Armenia, he developed a deep attachment to the country: "Armenia came to me in rugged chunks: rough hills and mountains; expanses of dry, non-irrigable land; pock-marked stone churches; eroding *khachkars* in rural cemeteries and churchyards, and massive sculptures." At the Genocide Memorial, the death of so many Armenians suddenly deeply affected him.

Garebian was born in Bombay, India, where his father chose to live after being reunited with his sister and met his future wife, an Anglo-Indian woman. "I was born a divided river beneath a bizarre zodiac. My father, a traumatized survivor of this century's first acknowledged holocaust; my mother, an Anglo-Indian, tributaries of her blood flowing from two directions."

It is fascinating to learn of Garebian's wide early reading and the deep influence of books on him. His memoir reads at times like a *Bildungsroman,* mapping his intellectual development. Like many young boys, he collected marbles and stamps, loved to play outdoor sports such as cricket and soccer, tried long-distance running, became an omnivorous reader—later referring to literature "my true country." Dorothy D'Souza, a neighbour from "The Retreat" where he lived, introduced him to popular novelists like Howard Spring, Pearl S. Buck, A.J. Cronin, and Neville Shute. Garebian mentions the Cambridge reading list that included Shakespeare, Dickens, Stevenson, and Scott, but nothing by Indian writers such as R.K. Narayan, Raja Rao, and Anita Desai. (These he would later discover in Canada.)

He benefited from his school's demand for "voluminous memorization," recalling having to recite such chestnuts as "Horatius at the Bridge," "The Charge of the Light Brigade," and "Sea Fever," which later helped him cultivate his talents for the theatre. He is critical of the fiction of Anglo-Indian writers such as Rudyard Kipling and John Masters: "I found Kipling's the hardest to accept because it was filled with vulgar Cockney soldiers and their bawdy barrack ballads." In contrast, he finds that E.M. Forster gave a more accurate picture of the complexities of Anglo-Indian society.

The topic of sex was not discussed in his home and certainly not in the all-boy school, St. Mary's, that was run by Jesuits. He speaks candidly about sexuality. He writes, "Like some of D.H. Lawrence's characters, I had sex on the brain as an adolescent."

From a North American perspective, it is difficult to understand the nature of his Indian birthplace. Garebian gives a detailed portrayal of Bombay with its ethnicity, race, and religion, remarking, "I did not glorify Anglo-Indian life; but nor did I seek Indian philosophy. I did not attempt to reduce India to a formula; but nor did I try to understand her enigmas."

Garebian describes the place where he lived at "The Retreat." At the back, there were small huts, broken down garages where the poorer classes lived. The houses formed three sides of the oblong compound with a huge rusting gate, never closed ... "When people spoke of "The Retreat" what they meant were the middle-class houses of accountants, store owners, teachers, public administrators." There were a wide variety of characters: "a smilingly polite family man, with camera slung over one shoulder, was, in fact, a brothel-owner and not a professional photographer. There was "Buffy" from Simla, who dressed like a man in tweed suits, puffed on cigars, and spoke in a deep voice," and the "Parsi sisters who lived with their extended family in a long, white villa, and who had a playboy bachelor-brother and a saintly other brother, the St. Francis of "The Retreat."

When the Garebian family was considering emigrating from India, his father wanted to choose England but had heard reports from Indian immigrants there was much racism there and his mother did not want to settle in "green but unpleasant England." Garebian writes, "So, Canada was chosen. Or chose us." The family immigrated to Montreal. He found the streets were much quieter and safer than Bombay. He thought Bombay was more communal, spiritual, filled with the vitality of social gatherings. But if Bombay had a rich diversity of culture, it also had a darker side where quarters were rife with crime, and he discovered Montreal was generally a safer city. He contrasts Montreal's sense of history to Bombay's by saying that it is particularly located in several historical sites, markets, statues, and buildings. In Bombay, history was everywhere: "History seeped into daily life."

Like many Canadian immigrants, the family's adaptation to Canada was not easy. Garebian wrote that his father felt a certain humiliation in having to return to manual work after being a manager in India, and his mother struggled against the cold and icy conditions getting to her job. His parents couldn't afford to send Garebian to university, so he decided to enroll in St. Joseph Teachers College. Sister Mary Desmond, who interviewed him was skeptical of his English abilities, but he later proved himself becoming the top student in Theology and English. The years at St. Joseph College allowed him to grow since he could cultivate his interest in theatre, producing and directing plays by Albee, Ibsen, Wilde, and

Shakespeare, as well as contributing articles to the college newspaper. Garebian graduated from St. Joe's *magnum cum laude*, won the Lieutenant-Governor's Medal, and delivered the valedictory speech.

From the age of 12, Garebian felt that he was destined to perform Shakespeare. He recalls, "I knew instinctively that Shakespeare was an artist of the highest degree ... Though an unparalleled genius, Shakespeare reflected some of the biases and ethical limits of his time. It seems unforgivably silly for a contemporary critic to view Shakespeare wholly through post-Holocaust, post-feminist and other 20th and 21st century Woke lenses, just as it is absurd to measure the morality of the Old Testament or the New by modern tenets."

Later he developed an even deeper interest in Shakespeare when he saw the famous British actor Sir Laurence Olivier on screen as Crookback, commenting that Olivier's performance was "dazzlingly spectacular, grotesquely comic, daringly seductive, thrillingly horrific," as Richard III or Henry V with "his trumpet voice ... rising to glorious heights of eloquent bravado," and the power and complexity of his presentation of Hamlet. "His protean technique enlarged a role imaginatively, revealing facets of character that other actors could never match."

He wrote a fan letter to Olivier and later Garebian managed to meet the great actor outside his dressing room in Montreal after Strindberg's *The Dance of Death*, and for once in his life, he admitted he was at a loss for words. Coincidently, I remember when I lived in London, England, in the late 1960s and worked for a summer as an usher at The Old Vic, Laurence Olivier also performing in Strindberg's *The Dance of Death*, and it was the best performance of an actor I've ever seen.

Garebian garnered experience in community and *ad hoc* theatre performing as Professor in Ionesco's *The Lesson*, the male lead of Henry Ghéon's *Passion Play*, and roles in T.S. Eliot's

Murder in the Cathedral. "They certainly helped me sense the moods of the audiences, as well as discriminate between good acting and bad." Garebian's producing, directing, and acting in theatre gave him first-hand experience and he used this knowledge as a reviewer and author of books on musicals and theatre.

At Sir George Williams University, later called Concordia University, he continued his research into Shakespeare. He was not impressed with some faculty members of Concordia's English department, composed of Americans who acted like "imperious neo-colonials," satirizing some of the faculty whom the students didn't like because of their idiosyncratic behaviour. When faced with obstacles or failures, Garebian responded with resilience when his thesis, a psychological study of Hamlet, was rejected because, he felt, of inadequate preparation and critical vetting by his academic advisor Leonard Mendelsohn; he quickly found a new supervisor, Michael Brian, and a new topic in which he researched the subjects of "Extravagance, Mediocrity, and Fire in *Hamlet* in order to show that the prince was not simply a victim of melancholy but of black bile or *choler dust*." This time his thesis was accepted.

Garebian is well known for his reviews, having penned over 1,200 of them. After reading many reviews in Canadian newspapers (*The Globe and Mail, The Toronto Star,* and the *Toronto Sun*), he became disturbed by their poor quality. When he submitted a review to the *Montreal Star*, Sheila Fischman reminded him, "But we are not the *New York Times*." Many of his reviews were about the productions at the Centaur Theatre in Montreal. He drew the ire of the director, Maurice Podbrey, when he wrote a review in *Performing Arts in Canada,* stating that English theatre in Quebec was becoming politically insignificant and cited examples of *Balconville, The Tomorrow Box,* and *Maggie and Pierre.* He did like several plays by Sky Gilbert, Diane Flacks, Daniel Brooks, George F. Walker, and

Hannah Moscovitch. He felt nationalism had become the "sacred norm" of our theatre. Podbrey disliked the article and removed Garebian from the reviewer's list. However, a year later, he was reinstated.

Concerning reviewing, he points out how notoriously little remuneration the reviewers received for writing, being paid only between 25 and 100 dollars for a review from 500-1000 words. This changed when the writer Heather Robertson brought a class action suit against over 350 corporations and publishers. The issue in unpaid compensation was resolved with a copyright settlement of 11 million dollars.

In the chapter "Thriving at Queen's, Languishing After," we learn that being on a one-year teaching leave, Garebian enrolled in the doctoral program in the English Department at Queen's University. After the challenging time at Concordia, he found the English Department at Queens a more positive and stimulating experience. Professor Norman H. Mackenzie wisely advised him to concentrate on Commonwealth literature as a subject for his dissertation as this might be more relevant and provide better chances in an academic career. Professor John Mathews enthusiastically urged him to study the Indian authors R.K. Narayan and V.S. Naipaul, and Garebian completed his doctorate in record time.

In the 1970s and '80s, Montreal was an exciting place for both French- and English-speaking writers, and Garebian recreates a sense of the culture and the atmosphere of his adopted city. He speaks in depth about his fascinating encounters with some of this period's most significant English writers. His freelance reviewing career bred some controversies. One of these concerned his *Gazette* review of *Poetry of the Seventies,* edited by Endre Farkas and Ken Norris, which argued that although the Véhicule Poets had a strong literary presence, the poetry generally wasn't of a high standard. After the publication of this review, he received letters of support from Irving Layton, Ralph Gustafson, and Henry Beissel. A pivotal point in his life occurred when he met the well-known and controversial poet Irving Layton, who encouraged him to write poetry, and this influential advice started him on the path of poetry. He admired Louis Dudek's excellent long poems *Europe, En Mexico,* and *Atlantis,* and Garebian also became friends with Henry Beissel, whose work attracted him because of "its dynamic investigations of histories, cultures, and contemporary issues."

Another significant writer who Garebian would meet was the well-known novelist and short story writer Hugh Hood. Garebian recounted an amusing situation when he was trying to learn to skate on an outdoor rink, and Hood came and offered him tips. They became friends in spite of his critical review of Hood's novel *The Swing in the Garden,* suggesting that the plot line was too "placid," and too concerned with documentary details, but generally speaking, Hood's short story collections impressed him, especially *Around the Mountain: Scenes of Montreal Life.* Hugh Hood became the subject of a Twayne's published work, *Hugh Hood* that came out in 1983; Garebian admitted that "it certainly put me on the literary map in Canada. In a small corner."

Garebian also admired another Montreal Story Teller, John Metcalf, because they shared similar critical positions and aimed for high critical standards in their work, and both disliked using nationalism as a barometer for critical taste. "As a polemicist and critic, he was caviar. I loved his acid wit and his courageous takedowns of some of the biggest overrated names in Canadian literature."

Garebian's real love, though, was writing about theatre—*Colours To the Chameleon: Canadian Actors on Shakespeare*—and he succeeds in communicating his ideas on roles, techniques, and authentic portraits of the actors. He wrote three books on the celebrated actor, William Hutt, conducted an in-depth interview with Heath Lamberts, and published articles on Nonnie Griffin, William Hutt, and Heath Lamberts in prestigious journals and encyclopedias.

In his book *William Hutt: A Theatre Portrait,* Garebian quotes Antoni Cimolino: "Almost impossible not to love such a person, an actor to the core, egotistical, vain, a bundle of anomalies"; an admirer of Noel Coward "he loved wit and could not help being witty ... His manner reminded me of Laurence Olivier." Cimolini called him "our true Northern Star."

Garebian writes, "Heath Lamberts was another genius." He was rebellious, quitting high school, did not quite fit in at the National Theatre School in Montreal, but later found his home on stage. He had wonderful talent as a comedian in his portrayal of Jourdain in Molière's *The Bourgeois Gentleman.* In his Cyrano, he could be "spry, elastic, wise, noble, melancholy, and heartbreaking, even as he made an audience laugh with him." Canada, Garebian wrote, could not understand Lamberts' genius, so he was forced, like many Canadian actors, to go to the States, where he gained recognition.

Another actress that Garebian had great respect for was Nonnie Griffin. Like Heath Lamberts, she had to go to the United States to find work. He praised her *Showbiz and other addictions*, "a genuine classic of theatrical and existential triumph over loss, unhappiness, and pain." She was adept at comedy, mimicking accents or using a memorable malapropism such as "He spent many years working on a caboose in Israel." Later in her life, she began to write one-act plays such as *Marilyn—After!* in which the audience could not believe they were not watching the real American legend. He wrote that Nonnie Griffin believed that acting not only emanated from the "mouth and throat" but the soul. She had the talent to epitomize a character by using only her voice.

A chapter in Garebian's life that I found particularly interesting was the one dedicated to his books. His career took a different turn when Jack David and Robert Lecker suggested that he consider doing a book on American musicals: *My Fair Lady, Gypsy*, and *West Side Story*. This was fortunate since he could do more research into one of his main areas of expertise, the theatre. He was able to use his own years of acting experience to go into books on theatre. *The Making of 'West Side Story'* and *The Making of Cabaret* (Second Edition) turned out to be among the most popular of Garebian's books, especially in the US market, and some of them found their way onto a reading list in American university courses.

One of the most fascinating aspects of Garebian's memoir came from the period after 2004 when he published his poetry books *Frida: Paint Me as a Volcano* (2004), *Blue*: *The Derek Jarman Poems* (2008), *Poetry Is Blood* (2018), and *against forgetting* (2019). Garebian wrote that he was one of only a few Canadian poets who synthesized poetry and theatre techniques. He demonstrated this in his next book, his bilingual *Paint Me As a Volcano*, the French poems excellently translated by Arlette Francière as *Un Volcan de Souffrance*. He wrote this book as a series of monologues in which he assumes the voice of Frida Kahlo and uses writing to showcase her Mestizo history, her involvement in politics and her relationship with Diego. In order to capture the spirit and life of Frida, he read Hispanic and Mexican poets, watched Spanish films, visited the Caza Azul, Kahlo's birthplace, and sites associated with her. He used his experience gleaned from theatre: "I approached my research as an actor would, probing beneath the surface of Frida's biography." Selections of the book were dramatized in a production by Jennifer Dale at the Cervejaria Restaurant in Toronto. He admits, "And then writing poems that would speak in the active present, vibrating like a soul in ecstasy or torment."

Regarding his next collection, *Blue: The Derek Jarman Poems,* he notes, "And it was inevitable that I would write about my own cultural and personal background." Garebian describes Jarman by trying to weave the writer's voice with his journals, which he found in the writer's art and films. Elana Wolff writes, "Even more than *Frida*, though, I would say Jarman presents as a kindred spirit—cinéaste, artist, sexual rebel, and gay rights activist. Brash, bold, provocative to the end." This book received glowing reviews.

In his next collection, *Children of Ararat*, Garebian wrote that this book derived from the Armenian sections in *Pain.* He wrote, "I was stung into poetry." He believed that people tend to forget suffering and that the world ignored the Armenian genocide. He wrote, "*Children of Ararat* seeks to illuminate *living* after and despite continuing terror, rootlessness, exile, ambiguities of identity." He also wrote this book to understand the artistic geniuses of Arshile Gorky, Sergei Paradjanov, Atom Egoyan, and William Saroyan; and it was a way of identifying himself as an Armenian.

In *Poetry Is Blood*, edited by Elana Wolff, he returns to the Armenian genocide. He speaks of an "ethical loneliness," and "from being a member of a persecuted group, has been abandoned by humanity, or by those who have power over one's life's possibilities." In this collection, he perceives grief not as an end but a place, a means of creating a "new reality of the self." He gives examples of writers such as Ocean Vuong, Billy-Ray Belcourt, Naomi Shihab Nye who depict suffering, indicating that through strong expressions language can produce beauty. He writes, "I can write of a legacy that rescues words within the hush of pillars, pediments, altars, urns, walls, monumental time." He concludes that the dead are not nameless, and that the writer must ensure that "they live in memory."

Garebian took the title *against forgetting* from Carolyn Forché's anthology of witness poetry. In this book, he attempts to interweave various fragments with Indian, Anglo-Indian, and contemporary history as he strives to find his own freedom through the act of not forgetting and by living through what is necessary to be remembered. He asks the reader to take an approach one would use in the theatre, "for a reader to sound my words, phrases, lines aloud" to get to their essence.

With every new book, Garebian discloses that he tries to "reinvent" himself. In the next two collections, he stays away from the poems of Armenia and India, but closer to home. *In the bowl of my eye,* is concerned with Mississauga and Etobicoke, people he has encountered, musing on the lake, park, and the neighbourhood. His next book, *Finger to Finger,* is his most confessional book. He delves there into his personal life, speaking of his two failed marriages and other relationships, his own sexuality, and growing older. He writes that he dares to become honest with himself, using Jack Gilbert as a model, confronting who he is, and acknowledging that those failures brought awareness into his life. Garebian mentions that he discusses the events of his private life in these poems. In my opinion, the memoir would have given a fuller portrait of his life if he had given us more details about his personal life, including his two marriages, along with the relationship with his son.

Garebian opens the final chapter by speaking of fighting cancer twice in eighteen years. He alludes to Louise Glück, who describes poetry as a "form / of suffering." He states that the awareness coming from suffering leads to "psychic growth," that we become more conscious of "relationships, creativity, aging, and mortality." Accompanying this sense of possible impending death, he discovered the stronger urge to live, quoting the American poet Joy Harjo, "even as we are dying something always wants to be born." If he felt weighed down by the disease, he drew his strength from writing poems out of his own vulnerability. He relates that he became more conscious of his surroundings, his senses more acute, even when he was undergoing cancer treatment, his mind developed a certain freedom to wander, to imagine what was "on the far side of existence." He began to reassess his life through his poetry. He could see the disease in terms of metaphors as his throat became "beggar's bowl, fire, a cup of wine, a wall gathering ghosts." He wondered, "What was it like to die?" The cancer treatment is very painful: "I would experience the worst pain and discomfort imaginable." Being agnostic, he could not turn to God for consolation.

After the cancer treatment was over, he travelled to Venice, Italy, and Thailand to find rejuvenation. He developed a different attitude, as suggested in Mary Oliver's line, "I walk in the world to love it." He writes, "As I advance deeper into old age, I hope I can find a relatively secure place from where I may proudly write another significant book and still make love ardently while discovering that I am, indeed, truly understood for what I write."

Keith Garebian's memoir, *Pieces of My Self,* showcases the writer's extraordinary life, whose sensibility and eloquence shine on every page. He weaves the various fragments of life into a whole, which deeply touch us. In the beginning, we witness a young man tormented by the grief of his father, who had lost most of his family members during the genocide of the Armenian people in 1915. We follow the writer's life's struggle to find his own identity and see how he was able to overcome difficulties and how surviving cancer helped him to develop an affirmative vision of life. Through continued persistence and dedication, he achieved his goals. Garebian's mind is powerful and dramatic, and his books map out a new perspective on the contemporary theatre scene and Canadian literature.

Voyeur or Witness? Keith Garebian's *Three-Way Renegade: $amuel $teward Without Apology*

JIM NASON

Imagine an old-fashioned recipe box—the kind of gunmetal-blue container where someone's grandmother keeps her favourite recipes for apple pie or Irish stew. Only there are no apples, potatoes, or carrots; instead, this rectangular box labelled Stud File, contains the salty details of hundreds of sexual encounters and the peppery sneezes of erotic secrets. Now imagine the details of those encounters in verse. In his *Three-Way Renegade: $amuel $teward Without Apology* (Frontenac House, 2023), Keith Garebian has created such a body of work.

Before we go into the shadowy world of Garebian's *Renegade*, let me take you back to a closeted me living in Calgary, Alberta, in 1979. After several rounds of beer at the Palliser Hotel, a friend suggests that he and I go to the Parkside Continental a few blocks away. Knowing that I like to dance, he tells me that they have the best music in the city. As we walk down Fourth Street he tells me that *the place is pretty wild. There are guys in dresses and you have to sign in to get through the door*. I don't ask what the *sign in* part is all about—I'm both curious and worried. It is common knowledge that if you are a 'homo' you are susceptible to being bashed, arrested, or blackmailed. I assume that a club deemed 'private' with a secret guest registry is less likely to be raided. But what will become of that registry? I wonder.

Moving forward a few decades, I hold in my hand and try to understand what motivated Garebian to write poems about the secretive sexual world catalogued so precisely by Samuel Steward (1909-1993). I open the book to the first poem and read about the *Meek little Methodist mama's boy from Ohio* who *prayed for a different puberty* and think back to my self-loathing coming out journey in Calgary. Although Calgary is a more enlightened city these days, one simply needs to look south of the border to know that human rights can shift on a dime—banning books with queer content and making it illegal to even use the word "gay" in schools is quickly becoming the norm in some states.

At the risk of spending too much time discussing American politics, the content of Garebian's book insists that I situate it within a social, political, and literary lineage that includes Whitman and other American poets who embody a non-traditional sexuality. I wonder what will become of queer poets like Carl Phillips, Mark Doty, and Henri Cole? I worry that Whitman's poems, with their blatant homoerotic content, will be removed from library shelves in the near future?

Garebian writes:

Walt Whitman's Calamus section,
blows up with massive TNT the staidly closeted English department,
Sam ignoring the fumes, inhales Clair (prof who glitters when he walks) (10)

Samuel Steward, the creator and guardian of the Stud File, was a writer of homoerotic novels and tattoo artist to movie stars and bikers. He also knew his poetry. He studied and taught literature for years and moved among literary circles that included Gertrude Stein and Thornton Wilder. He also trained as a librarian. I'm struck by the shape of Garebian's poems. Similar to Samuel Steward's Stud File, Garebian's poems are tight and consistent in size, each verse is about the size of a file card. They do not have titles. They are numbered, and sometimes work off the momentum of gossip, smut, and the promise of secrets revealed.

Garebian frames his book on the idea that Steward was a three-way renegade: a discontented literary academic, tattoo artist, and writer of pornographic literature who documented sexual encounters with hundreds of men, including Rudolf Valentino, André Gide, Tab Hunter, and Thornton Wilder. But why do any of us need to know what went on in bed between Samuel Steward and Rock Hudson (*faux hetero, Doris Day's pillow talk dreamy hunk*)? What was Garebian's need to pull back the sheets and expose encounters with hundreds of men under the guise of poetry? Perhaps the biggest clue Garebian gives us to assist in gaining a deeper understanding of this work arrives at the front of the book. He opens with a quote from John Ashbery: *Rather than be pure, accept yourself as numerous.*

This epigraph is the end of a line from Ashbery's poem "Some Words." Like most Ashbery poems, it is abstract, a surrealist painting of sorts, and is never meant to be read linearly or interpreted just one way. As a matter-of-fact, the book's title *The Double Dream of Spring*, is the title of a painting by surrealist artist Giorgio de Chirico on display in a gallery near where Ashbery lived.

The emotional tension held in poetry that draws from the shame of forbidden sexuality is like the sadist's whip ... the masochist wants more, the sadist, in possession of that information, holds back. Garebian provides both the sting and the soothing balm of unhinged secrets:

He scrubs away respectability, becomes renegade
specialist of the louche, greedy recorder of stats
and images, imprinting reminders of passions
as hopeful, hopeless as the world is. (28)

Motivated by research and ego, Samuel Steward's Stud File has the power to cause irreparable damage. In his writing on language, knowledge, sexuality, and power in his *Discipline and Punish*, Michel Foucault reminds us that knowledge is power, and the risk of punishment or incarceration is always near when you cross over the lines of social norms. The power inherent in Steward's detailed (and secret) Stud File put many at risk of losing their job, marriage, and/or family.

Weighing out personal safety while feeding sexual desires and being secretive about it all is not a new balancing act. Looking back to the 1981Toronto bathhouse raids I am aware of what can happen when people meet for sex in secret places. Toronto bathhouses were considered safe places where gay men could meet for anonymous sex and/or affection. For many they were a social haven away from the loneliness of the closet. Some of the men were married with children. Some of the men wrestled with religious faith or job status. Fondly referred to as Operation Soap by the officers who busted down doors and dragged occupants naked into police vans, the number of suicides and self-harming behaviours that came as a result of those raids deeply disturbs me. These are the transformative moments that prompt poets to investigate and write about the social structures and authoritarian practices that impact the lives of individuals living in marginalized communities.

As we read deeper into *Three-Way Renegade* Garebian enlightens us with the news that Samuel Steward was connected to some very influential literary figures. He brings us into the private lives of Gertrude Stein and Alice B. Toklas and reminds us that if you have enough money and status, you can get away with breaking the rules:

> *'Lovey' Gertrude in a kind of monk's*
> *cloth or burlap skirt, flat walking shoes. 'Pussy' Alice*
> *almost all in black, but for wild fruits and flowers in her hat. (42)*

Through Stein, Steward meets Thornton Wilder, twelve years his senior, and winner of the Pulitzer in both fiction and drama. *Thornton strikes a match on him.* Samuel Steward rallies on with his Stud File and Garebian's descriptions of individuals is masterful as Steward encounters Alfred Kinsey who shares his passion for recording sexual activity.

> *A 1949 knock on the door by Kinsey, solid, married, middle-aged,*
> *rumpled grey suit. Kinsey with greying buff-coloured hair,*
> *eyes sometimes blue, sometimes hazel, sensitive, wide mouth,*
> *prognathous jaw jutting out above a bow-tie. (62)*

In a book that discusses Steward's relationship with individuals such as Kinsey, it makes sense that Garebian's endnotes embody the tone and essence of scholarly research. As a poet with his own protracted 'coming out' journey, Garebian understands the pain of secrecy and the challenges (and joys) of living in various mindsets simultaneously. He also respects the need to enhance and validate his poems through research and documented reference. His endnotes present us with further prompters that propel us into Steward's elitist literary circles.

One of my favourite verses (128), resonates with John Ashbery. The sentences don't make much linear sense—yet, emotionally and rhythmically, they are profoundly logical. The final line is consistent with *Renegade's* themes of recklessness and restlessness: "*Animals will teach us what we can't teach ourselves.*" Endnote 61 reads:

> This poem is written in the manner of a cento, where each line is borrowed from a different poet, though I have made slight alterations in grammar in some instances. The quotations, line by line, are from Kenneth Koch, "Proverb"; John Koethe, "Sally's Hair"; Tom Sleigh, "At the Pool"; Meaghan O'Rourke, "The Window at Arles"; Stanley Kunitz, "Touch Me"; Mark Strand, "From Dark Harbor"; Sarah Manguso, "Hell"; and Thylias Moss, "There Will Be Animals."

Reading through the poems used to prompt Garebian's Cento further enriches the reader's poetic experience and adds substantially to the literary heft of this book. Garebian's poetic descriptions are breathtaking and brutal. An accomplished poet, his command of language as he describes Steward's search for connection among the loneliness of casual sex and hurt of unrequited love, is outstanding.

> *He wants those who want him back*
> *as if he wants more than they can hunger for*
> *more than lust dogging the heart.* (12)

Garebian describes an encounter with Alice Toklas after Gertrude Stein has passed away that is so honest and vivid the reader feels the Toklas loss, the irreversible of absence of Stein in her life.

> *... Allan, handsome, empty-headed ballet*
> *student, whom he takes to meet widowed Alice Toklas, humpbacked,*
> *diminished, weary, her moustache heavier, surviving anecdotally,*
> *in fur cloche down to her ears and with cane, not what she was.* (108)

And his portrayal of *small-minded USA* and the impact on gay men forced into hiding.

In airtight closets, where they die
without living how they fervently wish,
no thaumaturge to punch holes for clean air. (83)

Steward, as a tattoo artist, gains further access to numerous men. In his description of Steward's tattoo shop logo, Garebian echoes Gertrude Stein:

a rose with a phallic meatus at the center becomes his shop's insignia his official letterhead. This rose is not just a rose, not just a rose, not *just a rose.* (95)

Garebian elaborates on Steward's fondness for blue collar, rough-trade types, and sailors who came into his tattoo shop.

The sailor who knew far
sun and seas, bamboo huts, stone castles, crystal pools and sands,
dark blue skies and white stones, fountains and red-walled cities. (86)

With the confidence of a well-seasoned master poet, Garebian moves us through verse, writing one exceptional line after another:

no medievalist, he is worldly host to gay angels
and demons, his prized quantum being measurable sex. (91)

Elusive love glows chimeric, life stiffening with its bluffs. (96)

...flushes, blushes, / awe and shame, bricolage of the human. (100)

Although Samuel Steward was gathering material for his Stud Box long before Stonewall and the emergence in recent years of cruising/dating sites such as Grndr and Scruff, his 'research' and documentation bring up questions about behaviours deemed risqué even by the most liberal minded.

In *The Art of Daring; Risk, Restlessness, Imagination,* American poet Carl Phillips asks: "To put intimacy at risk, to put the body at risk—is this daring?" Phillips' poetry often discusses restlessness and risk; however, he continues, "more and more I think promiscuity's not daring at all, and not transgression—not when everyone can seem to be engaged in it, as indeed they seem to be, in the sauna, in the steam room, in the back room where the slings can be found. Or put it this way: the potential risk of promiscuity is to become cliché—the kiss of death for poetry; indeed for all art." (131)

Leaving the reader to wonder, once again, about Garebian's motive for writing these poems. Is he historian? Witness? Voyeur? As we move toward the end of the book, we encounter a narrator who *Yearns again for Paris:*

Where expats go who always want to live
excitingly. Where foreigners learn why Proust matters, and where
it's progress to change one's mind about many things. (107)

These lines resonate with Garebian's opening quote from Ashbery: *Rather than be pure, accept yourself as numerous* echoes. Perhaps Garebian is simply writing about a time in history when expressing one's innate sexual identity overtly could put a person at risk?

For months I worried about the Calgary man with the sign-in sheet at the Parkside Continental—what if he knew someone I worked with? What if he blackmailed me? What if he followed me home and beat the crap out of me? The cops certainly wouldn't have helped—often, they were the problem.

Without guessing or further complicating the book, I believe that the beauty of *Three-Way Renegade* resides in its archival sensibility and poems that make Garebian, once and for all, an exceptional poet who writes with the creative edge of a scholarly risktaker. Not risky in the way that Samuel Steward was, but risky in the discussion of complex social issues and human vulnerability.

In verse 111 we have an aging Samuel Steward that seems also to be saying something about an aging Garebian:

> *Cruel lines around his eyes in light, bulging belly,*
> *lilac wilting below the belt. Wrinkled confusion*
> *does not fade, nor armpits parched with secrets,*
> *as he gazes at sky, its clouds loose, his sighs*
> *sinking under sun.*

The cliché outcome of the lonely old tattoo artist and collector of secrets, the

> *Skin engraver who can ink anything but his heart ...*
> *the striptease, risking all,*
> *in cutting to the stem of love.* (117)

Garebian, *rising and falling with flair—lewd shape-shifting renegade*, borrows the lines of eight other poets and writes that Cento that takes us out of the world of whips and porn and brings us through the chaos of a grounded and nonjudgmental understanding of the books anti-hero, Samuel Steward:

Et les vivants sont dingues, the living are haywire.
It's like living in a lightbulb.
Climb into the light,
it turns you blind if you get hold of it.
Desire, desire, desire.
That does not change except for light.
The second-hardest thing is not be longing's slave.
Animals will teach us what we can't teach ourselves. (128)

In truth, Samuel Steward had tremendous power over the men he recorded. And, in reality, Keith Garebian, by transforming Steward's story into a book of poetry, has created a different kind of power that comes with hindsight and age. He writes with the clarity and authority that comes from years of writing poems and telling stories. *Renegade*'s strength resides in Garebian's willingness to write a complex biography in verse that doesn't withhold the unsightly or awkward. By peeking into Steward's Stud Files Garebian exposes something unique about people living on the edge of sexuality and gender/role identity:

... like Athena from Zeus's brow.
Heaven, earth, humanity in a triad
palpably in place for the three-way renegade. (119)

Garebian does not linger in last stanzas or definitive answers to questions about this book. A man who has lived a various and ever-changing life brings us an artistic mind, an all-embracing poetic sensibility. He refuses to be sentimental or moralistic. Whether one is motivated to engage the book as a reader of poetry or as a curious voyeur of eroticized history, the reader exits the pages equally shaken and enriched. By refusing to sleep in the great dullness of normal, Garebian has given us verse fueled by the erratic pulse of being fully alive:

> *... images worn*
> *away with the body's erasure, and the story's*
> *final words are not sensuous deviate delight.* (133)

Sources

Ashbery, John. *The Double Dream of Spring.* Ecco Press, New York, 1966.

Foucault, Michel. *Discipline and Punish: The Birth of the Prison.* Penguin, New York, 1975.

O'Hara, Frank. *In Memory of My Feelings.* Museum of Modern Art, New York, 2005.

Phillips, Carl. *The Art of Daring: Risk, Restlessness, Imagination.* Graywolf Press, Minneapolis, Minnesota, 2014.

against forgetting

A Review

ELANA WOLFF

"A poem can hold more mysteries more easily than any factual timeline," writes Naomi Shihab Nye—2019-2020 Young People's Poet Laureate of the Poetry Foundation of Chicago. Nye's line aptly describes the holding-effect of Keith Garebian's intricate documentary voice in *against forgetting* (Frontenac House, 2019)—a collection of twenty-eight poems comprising the fourth volume of what might be called a 'Tetralogy of Witnessing and Becoming'. In these pieces Garebian revisits the ground of his combined histories—the barbarized Armenia of his father, the Anglo-Indian heritage of his mother, the multicultural Bombay society of his childhood, and his journey to maturity in Canada—"repeat[ing]," as he writes in the introductory Note, "a narrative that implies connections it does not explicitly state."

Garebian's earlier explorations into this fraught autobiographical territory are covered in *Pain: Journey Around My Parents* (Mosaic Press, 2000), a book of meditations, anecdotes, historical narrative, literary commentary, and prose poems that represent his first coming to grips with the trauma of extremity; in *Children of Ararat* (Frontenac House, 2010), a personalized 'witnessing' and 're'/membering of the 1915 Armenian genocide; and in *Poetry Is Blood* (Guernica Editions, 2018), a tour-de-force passage into multivalent poetics demonstrative of deep generational upheaval. With a*gainst forgetting*, Garebian rounds out, as it were, the 'tetralogy' in a sage and "unglazed" portrait—from birth to present—of "soul trying to break through / words ... peculiar slant of memory, / inclinations of surfaces, / enchantments of the self," striving against forgetting, toward integration.

The opening poem, "Forgetting"—prefaced with an epigrammatic definition of 'forget'—verbalizes the deliberative thematic tone of the work. In the folio verso piece, "Ways of Forgetting," readers are reminded, grammatically, that remembering and forgetting "have conditionals," are "factual and contrafactual," "real and unreal." Which is to say that remembering can be hypothetical, "partial," "wrong," "mismanaged," even creative. Things fade, details get lost, concealed, and "desires build new tissue." "The curious past grows curiouser," puns Garebian in closing the poem—quipping both memory and Anglo-enchanter Lewis Carroll together with his plucky heroine Alice who cried "Curiouser and curiouser," so surprised by the transmutations of her travels she forgot (as if) "how to speak good English."

Garebian's palette is expansive. In "Fire," the forces of the author's birth are both geographical —"born near water"; and astrological—"Cancer, my first memory is fire." The personal is plural too: "In Bombay, fire was common, communal: / Zoroastrians prayed facing the sun ... / Hindus worshipped Agni." And the elements are mutual, even as they're individualized: "Fire a beast whose fierce breath / lived in me," Garebian proclaims, "I could hear the portentous. / I did not know then what I would / be saying of it." Water and fire serve destiny—as thematic through-lines and aspects of constellations of pain. In "Torment"—flash-forward to Canada—Garebian finds elemental mutuality in the company of other immigrants: "In the 60s, I taught boat people, / whose adolescent minds couldn't shake off sea water ... the acrid / memory of smoke and flame." The experiences of water, smoke and flame differ for teacher and student, yet from the teacher's perspective, they're connective. Grief is expressed as deeply-embedded, empathically felt.

The fire theme is personalized further in "Reading Ashes," with the opening line "My parents, chronic smokers / ... He, the one cremated, / remains in a gleaming urn"—"urn" providing the ecumenical reminder that "*you are dust, / and to dust shall you return.*" Garebian's strongest voice is declarative, commemorative, also rhetorically interrogative. In the poem "Autobiographical Whispers," "Question of origins is smoke. / We can always be somebody else / behind a smokescreen." Here he touches on a motif that's given specifically artistic treatment in his collection, *Frida: Paint Me As a Volcano* (BuschekBooks, 2004); namely that of the mask as expression of authentic and plural identity. We are never one just one identity, and even our 'smoke-screened' personae can be real if we save the appearances. In "How I Was Made," Garebian quotes Gertrude Stein in service of what is saved / remembered: "...you are never yourself to yourself except as you remember yourself." What Garebian remembers is "spasmodic ... slant, never fully of a single place."

The poems in a*gainst forgetting* are laid out like memory—in point / counterpoint, detail / association; chronologies compressed and intermixed. In the pivotal piece, "The Retreat," an "Old Victorian house ... / with a compound gate never / closed" evokes the formative impact of first residence. The poem rehearses the multiple influences of Garebian's childhood socio-cultural matrix: "Pathan, Goan, Marwari, Anglo-Indian, / Hindu, Muslim, Irani, Parsi, / Catholic, Jew." "Anglo-India" extends this thread: "Always part of someone else's story ... Anglo-India ached / for lost glory, choked in dervish / dust." Garebian's bequeathal is one of intermingling and toleration, also of colonial injustice, ethnic subordination, and the will to overcome. In one of the most poignantly personal pieces, tellingly titled "Pigment," he closes with a candour that alludes to a layered, deeply-rooted father-son conflict as well: "My father worried my skin would darken / if I played too much cricket or soccer. / What whiteness could be added?"

In Water," as "a diarist of water," Garebian circles back to his boyhood Bombay: "Having been born near water, I have read / water ... Water's own bright grace, my element ... Fishermen were here before the English." The vital line is: "Where had the sea been before the land appeared?" Here he intones at his most expansive—the inference being that we are all from elsewhere before we are from here—wherever here is. Even the land is from elsewhere, even the water. In other words, otherness and displacement are as existential and universal as arrival and departure; as ubiquitous as becoming and unbecoming.

In "Second Country," where "snow and ice replace heat and dust," Garebian affirms that in Canada he "feels safer ... there is no more Empire, just colonial residue ..." Canada is a country where "poetry changes nothing," he asserts. Except that poetry has, by his own admission, affected his own personal unfolding. In an interview, he once told me that he's freer than his father was ever able to be, because he has given voice on the printed page to 'witnessing' his parents' histories and his own—something they were never able to do.

The long and summative closing poem, "Self-Portrait in a New World," celebrates a life's g/leanings. Herein Garebian pays homage to peers, poetry mentors, and works that have touched, influenced, and indeed, changed him. He names Olivier and Shakespeare, quotes *Coriolanus* and *Othello*, American poets Jorie Graham, John Ashbery and Ocean Vuong; cites Dante as more valuable than Derrida, and nods to Anne Michaels in the line "the weight of water, the cost of oranges." "Literature kept me sane," he maintains. "Though stories and poems ended, / their shadows never vanished, / my world changed with their changes." In reaching the last line, one grasps the mysterious sense that "The past is here," held in heart, memory, and printed word.

Interview with Keith Garebian for Open Book, 2020

ELANA WOLFF

Elana Wolff: Let's begin with your recent collection of poems, *against forgetting* (Frontenac House, 2019). In preparing to review this collection, I came to viewing *against forgetting* as the fourth volume in what I termed "A Tetralogy of Witnessing and Becoming." As the son of an Armenian father (and Anglo-Indian mother), you've been brought into personal / next-generational proximity of a trauma of extremity; namely, the Armenian genocide of 1915. You first explored this fraught auto/biographical ground in *Pain: Journey Around My Parents*, published in 2000. You returned to the same territory in *Children of Ararat* (2010), *Poetry Is Blood* (2018), and again in *against forgetting*. Can you speak to the ongoing pursuit of this subject-matter. What have you returned to, to address? What was left unsaid in the first and second volumes that brought you to a third, and most recently to a fourth?

Keith Garebian: Like many immigrants and expatriates, I feel I am often out of place even after having found one literally in Ontario. This is my exilic sense—a feeling that no matter where I settle, there is a deep-rooted melancholy for what exactly I do not know. Perhaps it is something inherited from my Armenian side. Armenians today are a scattered people. However, most have developed a sense of belonging to wherever they have put down new roots. I have put down roots in Canada, but I often feel like a "resident alien" (to use Clark Blaise's phrase). I have always been a divided being: one part Armenian; a small part English; another small part Indian; and a fourth part Canadian. The proportionality is, of course, indecipherable, if no other reason than that every part bleeds into another, making it all but impossible to measure percentages. Not that I would ever really want to do so, because in a profound sense each of us is unfinished, incomplete. We can never know who we really are because it is impossible for us to see ourselves the ways others see us. As a writer, I like ambiguity, a little vagueness. It lends a sense of existential mystery, as well as drama. It becomes a spur to act towards self-definition, without expecting full disclosure or closure.

As I am most often characterized as half Armenian and half Anglo-Indian, I find it insightful to investigate the implications of such division. I am presently at work on an autobiography that I have titled *Pieces of My Self* in implicit recognition that autobiography is really rhetoric generated and organized to give voice to something that issues from a psychic centre. In telling my story, or important parts of it, I am inescapably telling a story of Armenians and Anglo-Indians, with my personal history possibly conjoined with the history of collectives. I do not mean to suggest, however, that I represent a collective or speak for one. I simply mean that my personal story is linked in some way with their stories. This is both a blessing and a burden as I strive to be true to myself as a writer despite aesthetic and political pressures on me.

Although language is really my home, I know that words and metaphors are not enough to restore the psyche to a place of equilibrium. But language does strengthen my lyrical capacity, stretch my mind and imagination, help me give voice to the voiceless, allow me to speak of different tribes, and enable me to articulate my identity (literary and psychic).

I become most Armenian (despite not speaking, reading, or writing the language) when reviving some parts of Armenian history, memorializing the Armenian past, and questioning the Armenian Diaspora while promoting it.

Similarly, I remain Anglo-Indian (despite having left India as a teenager, without ever returning) by recalling Anglo-Indian history and interrogating its dwindling value. And, then, as a Canadian (would I still be a New Canadian at my age?), I have learned new texts, new literary influences, without finding harmony between the land and my reflections of and about it.

With reference to my books after *Pain* and *Children of Ararat*, I can say that *Poetry Is Blood* and *against forgetting* are both concerned with expulsion, departure, exile. In *Pain*, my mother was the opposite of my father: she was an Anglo-Indian who never questioned the historical, sociological, political, or cultural implications of this identity, whereas he, having been orphaned as a little boy and not having found a relatively secure second home till he learned English, a useful trade, and established himself in Bombay, without ever feeling fully at peace, was never really rooted. He was Armenian, which means he came from an ancient land and civilization that was not exclusive. Armenia was an ancient empire but then, as with every empire, it shrank, became diluted by invading cultures, and then became nearly extinct. To survive, it had to be ready to accept mutability, cope with near-annihilation, perennial external political threats, and internal fission. *Poetry Is Blood* is, in many ways, a book for my father who, by the end of *Pain* and *Children of Ararat*, was a flawed hero to me. *Pain* was written out of painful love, not condemnation. As perceptive reviewers and readers noted, it is a memoir in which I struggle to know and love him for all his flaws and for our squandered opportunities to know, understand, forgive each other for the wrongs each had done to the other. Two very close Armenian family friends of ours were shocked at how much I *hated* him in the book, seriously misreading the text. *Pain* is not about hate for my father at all. I have never ever written a book dedicated to such a destructive passion. Serious, open-minded and open-hearted readers would discover this if they reread the memoir, particularly the last seven pages carefully, but, alas, the book has long been out of print. Therefore, allow me to sum up my position by quotations:

We, who have never suffered as much and know only the names for such pain, tolerate images as livid as wounds. We may spend our days writing of the dead and then find consolation at night in quiescent sleep.

He, however, never learned to write of poised or wrenched life. He had seen too much in his first history lesson, his tortured boyhood, to know what to select and articulate in the next.

We did not know how to share his pain, how to make it as intimate as love.

Here is another passage: "His history had been an aching wound, and I had always wanted to look into this wound more closely, though I felt, as his years fell into the yellow leaf, uneasy about drawing closer to him. His dark side, his wildness had been overwhelming." And following this: "Age and experience, however, have taught me that our fathers alone don't fully give us their wounds."

When my father died, my grief was mixed with relief: "He and I would no longer be pulsing contraries, each stubborn with a faith in different infinities. He and his murdered tribe were now ever-receding soundwaves in our uncertain galaxy, whereas I was left to find a voice for his history and my future."

In the same vein, there is this: "He died without ever telling me if he had retained any faith in man, but I know instinctively that he willed for me a survival against despair. He never said aloud whether he thought a writer disappeared so much into imagination as to be absent from the real world, but I know in my bones that he wished for me to find a place in whatever world where I could bear witness to a devastation of grace."

And that voice spoke in *Children of Ararat*. This collection (expertly edited by the late Mick Burrs before the wonderful Rose and David Scollard at Frontenac House finalized the editing) was divided into four parts, the first of which dealt specifically with my father, whose name was Adam and for whom the Armenian genocide must have been experienced as a new Fall of Man. He was dispossessed of home, lost both his parents, and two younger sisters, and had almost his entire family history erased. I never knew his parents or sisters, so I had to imagine what they must have endured, and poetry became my express vehicle for imagining those traumas and losses. It is instructive for readers to know that one of the final poems in the first section is entitled "I Have Inherited You," which links to all I have said above.

The second section of the collection is deliberately horrifying as it details forms of atrocity. Filled with rage, it does not pretend to be subtle or oblique because its themes transcend literary politesse or euphemism. It is poetry of vicarious witness, without filters. I guess it is similar to some of the passionately didactic poems of Layton and contemporary black and gay/lesbian/transgender poets. I see a connection between the very explicit poems, "Two Photographs," "Tattooed Girls, Part One," and "Tattooed Girls, Part Two," and photographs of torture, victimization, and murder. Susan Sontag once famously asserted that people "want the weight of witnessing without the taint of artistry, which is equated with insincerity or mere contrivance." I wasn't aware of her statement at the time I wrote those poems, but now I can use her words in defense of my strategy. A poetry critic could wonder "Where does poetry live?" in such writing. My response would be "In poetic language, whatever the impulse and emotional pressure." Like many other poets in other languages, I am a poet of human details, who never ceases arguing with history or theology. And in companionship with other Armenian poets (even those who write only in Armenian), I am resolutely in the camp of the near-annihilated, the deracinated, the dispossessed, the exiled. This accounts for my empathy for Palestinians, First Nations people, and any people who have been unhoused, uprooted, denied their rightful freedoms, identities, and homes.

The third section has more craft as it explores through ekphrastic poems great Armenian painters, filmmakers, and writers, such as Arshile Gorky, Sergei Paradjanov, Atom Egoyan, William Saroyan. This was a crucially important section, but one that hardly any critics bothered to engage with in either a didactic or aesthetic way. I guess it did not fit their preordained categories of form or investigation.

The fourth and final section encapsulates some of the urgencies of Armenian psychic, cultural, geographical, and moral burdens. It repeats the image of history as a colophon that first arose in *Pain*, with a new understanding of the metaphor in the light of Paul Celan's explanation of poems heading toward "some open place that can be inhabited, toward a thou which can be addressed, perhaps toward a reality which can be addressed." Denial, in the way Turkish history continues the theme and practice, is a historical and moral vice. *Children of Ararat* is my lyrical way of comforting a people filled with insecurity and doubt. We all have the right to dream that denial will run to its own ruin, though it is only a dream as yet. I keep remembering Nick Thran's contention that the Afterword "collapses into prose." I have never considered prose to be a declension of poetry. An Afterword is meant to be in prose, just as a Foreword would be. Ironically, the Afterword was originally meant to be the Foreword, but on the advice of Peter Balakian I shifted it to the end. Thran's review was, on the whole, thoughtful but it hardly encompassed my craft. I know I am going to sound like Irving Layton trumpeting his own genius, but I absolutely believe that there are many poems in this collection that would not be out of place in Carolyn Forché's landmark anthology of international poetry of witness *Against Forgetting*.

The fact of Armenians being a minority everywhere outside the Republic of Armenia (which is but a tiny part of a once huge, once-great empire) is a story of victimhood that has not had much of a chance to be told widely in poetry written in English. In the U.S. there is, of course, the poetry of Peter Balakian, the greatest Armenian writer in the English language, who has mastered various forms: collage poetry, the essay, and documentary history. Before him there were William Saroyan and Diana der Hovanessian: the former, of course, greater; the latter, whose greatest contribution was by way of Armenian poets. But I am not familiar with any American Armenian of note who has tried or is trying to make despair and dispossession poetically strong. In Canada, Lorne Shirinian had to publish his own poetry to give voice to the camp of historical "losers" or victims. Shirinian showed a capacity to compose the Armenian presence in Canada. And I have come along in my own way, in my own time, to expand that capacity while being alone within myself.

I don't believe in pure races. I don't believe in simple categories of victors and victims. I have been enriched by being multi-racial, by having inherited aspects of ancient civilizations (India and Armenia), as well as by being open to an intermingling of ethnicities and cultures in India and Canada. Echoing the great Palestinian poet Mahmoud Darwish, I can affirm that there is no ghetto in my identity. Born in a

South-Asian country, whose national language I do not speak, born into English, language of a colonial empire, unable to read the ancestral language of my own father, transplanted to a second country whose contemporary poets (except for the Indigenous, Asian and black immigrants, and gay, lesbian, transgender practitioners) often eschew emotionality in favour of prevailing post-modernist techniques, I often feel an urgency in my poetic vocation. I seek to link voices, fields, distinct contexts in a sonorous manner. I allow poppies, pomegranates, plates, Ararat, darkness, orphaned children, tools, paintings, films, books their own voices as relics of history. I speak in their name because they are denied a speaking voice or concrete language. I believe in lyricism and cadence. I celebrate my passion for sounds, my inclination to be musical with language. I think this tendency was first manifested in monologue form in *Frida: Paint Me As a Volcano* and, more strongly and versatilely, in *Blue: The Derek Jarman Poems.* And those two collections were not Armenian in any way, except, perhaps, for an underlying melancholy, a peculiar lamentation, charged with cadence rather than conventional metre. I realize that melancholy and lamentation are not qualities that apply only to Armenians, but I feel that my poetry has a personal cadence because of a personal sense of feeling *odar* or the Other virtually anywhere, of having a surname whose etymological root is probably Arabic or Turkish (*garip*) without exact English translation, and one that connotes apartness, strangeness, or a degree of alienation.

With all these ideas churning within me, I sought to rehearse and flout conventions of lyric poetry in *Poetry Is Blood*, a collection you so expertly edited at Guernica. This book has a wide cross-stylistic reach: lyric, list poetry, anti-lyric, fetish of last lines, dialogue, aborted or unfinished lyric. Divided into four parts, its themes range from family history and tribal history/culture to emblematic example and existential philosophy. The very first poem of four lines "April" (which you helped me sculpt out of a much longer, wandering poem) situates the theme of memory. And the next poem is also a memory-poem, but this one is an imagining of my father as a boy. Next comes a compressed autobiographical poem involving my father and me in our conflicted relationship. And then there are other family poems. Within all of these is a strong current of melancholy, sometimes bitter, crystallized in the anti-lyric "A Bird Cries in an Orchard." As no critic has as yet noted, this one has a circularity while being a calm unfolding with obsessive repetition. There is something vaguely Oriental in its shape and cadence. There are strange poems, too, such as "Errata," which is a list poem with sharp connotations, each word on the list alluding to historical genocide and its resulting trauma. And what I said earlier about naming comes to a head in the first section with "Title Search," which is an assemblage of specific titles by real Armenian authors relating to Armenian history and culture. Even this one is shaped with cadence.

As I am the poet being interviewed here, I do not want to keep up a commentary, but in the interest of indicating how I am not simply a documentary or didactic poet, let me point readers to other experimental poems in this book. "Okra" is not just about food. It is about ingesting the implications of a name, a father-son dynamic. "A True Portrait of Talaat Pasha" parodies Gertrude Stein in imagining a (whispered?) sinister monologue by a real-life arch perpetrator of genocide and denial. "They Had Some Rugs" owes its inspiration to Joy Harjo, the first Native American to serve as Poet Laureate. It uses an Armenian emblem to encapsulate an entire people's tragedy. "Finishing Sentences" is the most difficult poem I attempted in the collection because it deploys aborted syntax in a concentration of urgencies. Its rush of language imparts a sense of something perpetually becoming or changing as it moves, its phrases rising and falling with an internal logic calibrated to the magnitude of its subject. Finally, with the last poem in the book, "Fetish of Last Lines," I use only the final line from individual poems in the collection to sum up the principal direction and final meditation, "Between unsaying and forgetting, / how each of us becomes void / in any land. / There is only the earth."

So, *Poetry Is Blood* is at once wide-ranging and deeply personal. Long after it was published, I happened to read Mahmoud Darwish's interviews in *Palestine as Metaphor* which articulated certain things that my own poetry aspires to being. Darwish claims that "the humanity of man began with his apprenticeship of names." An obvious enough point, dating back to Adam naming God's creation, but in my case, the naming has autobiographical and tribal motives. In *Poetry Is Blood* I introduce Armenian names of monuments, ancient walls, paintings, martyred poets, and historical tragedy into Canadian poetry in English. By recollecting these names—Deir ez-Zor (the Armenian Auschwitz preceding Auschwitz), Garni Temple, Diyarbakir, Siamanto, Komitas, Nagash the Ghareeb (note the sonic similarity with my own surname), the Genocide Monument, and other submerged names that are present through allusion—I join in humanity's perennial song of recollection, lamentation, and nostalgia. I really do believe that my own "songs" are a part of this broad, international song, linking me with Sayat Nova, Siamanto, Komitas, Saroyan, Goran Simic, Mahmoud Darwish, Yehuda Amichai, Irving Layton, Henry Beissel, Paul Celan, Gottfried Benn, Anna Akhmatova, Osip Mandelstam, Joseph Brodsky, Max Jacob, Gunter Eich, Cesare Pavese, Charles Simic, Primo Levi, Constantine Cavafy, Yannis Ritsos, Derek Walcott, Ocean Vuong, Billy-Ray Belcourt, Kevin Irie, Joy Kogawa, and many, many others.

I do not make this claim lightly or breezily. I do not intend to elevate my own importance. I do, however, wish to clarify my poetic intent and practice. I wish Canadian critics and academics could think outside their rigid boxes, the ways poets can. I wish they would not shrink from lyricism as if it were a pathological condition. I wish they recognized that there is an amplitude of ways by which to bear witness across generations and cultures, and by which the poetic imagination can make the past urgent, as Peter Balakian does. I would also like these critics and academics to rethink their clichés about lyric and epic. There needn't be a contradiction between these two terms, as Darwish has shown. Traditional heroic themes are exhausted on some levels. We live in a modern, anti-heroic world where collective tragedy is developed or expressed only through a complex of individual tragedies—as in genocides or attempted genocides. Therefore, the poems in *Children of Ararat* and *Poetry Is Blood* billow into something larger than the individual poems. I have poems about particular tragedies: my maternal grandmother's death from starvation and a broken heart; my traumatized father; Armenian children blinded by infected water during their exodus; tattooed Armenian girls raised as slaves or chattels; Arshile Gorky's mother, his paintings, his suicide; William Saroyan's trauma; the murder of Hrant Dink; Egoyan's archives of intimacy; broken bodies in Deir ez-Zor; Armenian poet-martyrs, and others. It isn't a matter of accumulating statistics. It is a question of linking microcosms of destruction to a macrocosm of atrocity. I raise the question, "where is the precision / of headless bodies, of unmarked graves, / shreds of scarves hanging on walnut trees, / of apple-cheeked children / whose golden hair was carried/ by winds to the mountains?" Sensory details of things to be felt, smelled, tasted, all combined with the sense of something individual or particular expanded into the universal.

My multi-racial ancestry frees me from being imprisoned within high walls of language. The fact that I write only in English is paradoxically liberating because English by being a hybrid language is capable of absorbing the Other. The other way of saying this is, as Darwish puts it, "Perhaps the English language is more 'imperialist' than others."

against forgetting, sensitively edited by Micheline Maylor, is an autobiographical narrative sequence that incorporates discrete lyrics within a unified whole. The title is borrowed from Carolyn Forché, and it prompted me to recognize some of the key features in my narrative: progression *but* incompleteness. As I proclaim in my Author's Note, "The discrete poems (with their wounded and wounding words) are circumscribed by the larger narrative of my Bombay background and immigration to Canada, with all the attendant issues (such as cultural and psychic identity, displacement, voluntary exile or expatriation, and the feeling of alienation) that do not make for a tidy closure." Al Moritz's superb blurb helped entice other readers, and your review in the League of Canadian Poets newsletter was the first in-depth one I received in print. Laurence Hutchman claims that I am a brilliant thinker, but I don't see myself in those terms. I think, therefore I am, of course. But my thinking is not systematic, and my poetry does not seek to be cerebral. I turn poetry inward. I read a lot of international poetry in English, and I align myself more with contemporary American poets than others because they are unafraid of expressing emotion in ways that defy received literary conventions or established forms. I think very highly of Jericho Brown and Ocean Vuong, for instance, just as I do of Mark Doty, Terrance Hayes, and Edward Hirsch.

But to return to *against forgetting*. I no longer see a need to keep exploring the father-son dynamic I covered in prose and poetry earlier. I no longer see a need to show my Armenian roots. My earlier collections cover that ground amply. Moreover, it is sad to admit this, but the Armenian community in Canada, at least as I have experienced it in Toronto, is not given much to poetry, certainly not poetry in English. It doesn't seek to open itself to poetry that is not exclusively about Armenian subjects. I find this not only sad, but ironic, given that the mother country reveres its ancient poets. Perhaps this community does not see a need to participate in a wider human landscape via poetry. Perhaps there is a fundamental misunderstanding or ignorance of what poetry can achieve, over and above history. But I can only hope that this community will some day come to know and understand the radical truth of Mahmoud Darwish's dictum, "A people without poetry is a conquered people."

against forgetting is filled with history, not just my own as an Anglo-Indian or of the British in India, but of world history, as in poems about Vietnam under imperial American attack, Armenian history, and the Jewish genocide in Europe. These poems about some of the effects of war exist in the shadow of other wars not named or mentioned in the book, such as in Africa or the Middle East. And one of the biggest wars is the most personal one, pertaining to my war with myself over ethnicity, identity, immigration, citizenship. The book attempts to portray my own origins, how I was made, and why I have never felt fully of a single place.

against forgetting expresses a complex knot of personal and historical fact and argumentation. Although I have represented my divided racial and cultural identity in other books as well, I never speak as a representative of a whole group. I write poems not as a "we," but about myself as part of certain groups. I never wear a "we" mask, although there is the final line in "Finishing 33 Sentences" (from *Poetry Is Blood*), "But we are the Mountain, so," which is a fragment, not a complete sentence for several reasons. In this concluding fragment of that poem, I am suggesting an unfinished story but one that manages to proclaim the continuing strength of endurance and survival, despite a history of violation, uprooting, deracination, brutality, attempted annihilation by a criminal perpetrator. I am not a national poet, but I imagine myself having different voices of different cultures. I sometimes certainly try to express the *spirit* of a people—Anglo-Indian or Armenian. If anything, I have been looking for a place in history while recognizing that my own history is marked by loss—on the Armenian and Anglo-Indian sides of it. This implicit and explicit sense or feeling is what makes me a poet of brooding melancholy in my three most personal poetry collections: *Children of Ararat*, *Poetry Is Blood*, and *against forgetting*. And when you add my memoir *Pain* to the group, you do have, as you have astutely pointed out, a tetralogy of witness about who and what have been experienced as loss.

EW: You've given a long and richly detailed answer, Keith. Very generative! In most direct response to my initial question, you speak of being presently at work on an autobiography that gives voice to your "psychic centre"—of which an important part is being an Armenian/Anglo-Indian, conjoined to the history of a collective. So, I suppose that the short answer to my first question is that you really are not completely done with the ground of the tetralogy. There's more to be plumbed, even though you also say that you "no longer see a need to keep exploring [your] Armenian roots." I suppose there's a certain tension between need and deeper need, as it were ... You speak of *Palestine As Metaphor*, the 2019 collection of interviews with poet Mahmoud Darwish, of how Darwish's thoughts in these pieces resonate with your own. I'm wondering if you view, with Darwish, the "past as undying?" And if this is part of what keeps you linked to it? You relate that you don't speak Armenian, cannot read Armenian poets in the original. You lament that the Armenian community in Toronto "is not given much to poetry, certainly not poetry in English." You also relate that you have not returned to India since immigrating to Canada in your youth, though you're an avid traveller. So, if not linguistic or physical return to your formative past, I'm wondering if psychic memory is part of what you seek? And/or, with Darwish, a kind of 'inter-immersion' ... Darwish states emphatically that he is "Arab, for he speaks Arabic," and yet he wants to "live all cultures." He names Canaanite, Hebraic, Greek, Roman, Persian, Ottoman, French, and English, as well as Arab. I'm sensing that this kind of cross-culture embrace might be what you are pointing to, at least in poems in *against forgetting*: "The Retreat," in which you poeticize and celebrate the multiple cultural influences of your childhood in Bombay, and in "Water," which brings the inference that we are all from elsewhere before we're from where we are. It seems to me that there's a source for deep empathy in this piece—the notion that we are all in some way Other and that otherness, dis/placement, deracination (psychic and/or physical), as well as justice and injustice are existential and dialectical.

KG: As with every collection of mine *against forgetting* strives to show that poetic form is not immutable. I wanted to show how colonized experience can turn you into "a wider nation." But first, I wanted to express sensations of uprooting, diaspora, and identity through conscious means. These issues are psychic ones, in addition to being sociological, political, cultural questions. They are often the result of wars or strife in a political sense, but they could also be a result of private wars. One of the biggest wars is the most personal one, pertaining to my war with myself over ethnicity, identity, immigration, citizenship. The book attempts to portray my own origins, how I was made, and why I have never felt fully of a single place. It rehearses many of the themes raised in *Pain*, so in a sense, it completes an autobiographical circle. But the circle is not neatly drawn. There are erasures along the circumference, teasing gaps that are meant to suggest the ambiguity of my identity. Or as one poem puts it in its own title, "Holes to Be Filled." Words such as "Past," "Broken," "Now" establish a temporal dynamic, with "Now" being "*in media res* of a narrative / with boundary issues."

You may be correct in thinking that I am not done with the ground of the tetralogy, though at the moment I am working on parts of an autobiography in which I am very aware of a push-pull dynamic at work in the text. When I arrived with my parents and two younger sisters in Canada in 1961, I became aware that my accent and way of speaking was quite different from that of Canadians. I did not wish to seem exotic, yet I wanted to be considered separate in an essential way. I had English, the Bible (as mythology), Shakespeare, and the Commonwealth as my commonalities with Canada, but in a subconscious way, I was Other, not totally or even superficially alike my peers at college. At the beginning, I dressed differently (more conservatively), had different tastes in reading, fine art, film, and theatre. Let me quote from the work-in-progress, which I have titled *Pieces of My Self*, though the title could eventually change. "I did not want to sound tonally flat in speech. I was never a conformist, so I did not wish to look like 'one of the gang' anywhere. At the same time, I did not want to be reminded how different I was from my peers. This push-pull tendency wrinkled my life significantly, making me feel incomplete. My father looked and sounded like an immigrant, with his workman's cap and heavily accented, mangled English. He was embarrassing enough because I felt uneasy about inviting new friends into the home. My curiosity and my language were far wider than his, although he was not a man for whom his own life was the only story. He cared about us, though he felt humiliated having to return to manual labour as an automobile mechanic after having been the equivalent of vice president of a car factory. And there were no servants in Montreal to reinforce his status or ease the domestic life of my mother. There was no clan for him to claim as his own in Montreal—not till he discovered the Armenian community, but he felt out of place even with the few members he got to befriend.

My mother, too, felt out of place. Compelled by a radical change in economic fortune by our immigration, she returned to the work force, her age and long professional inactivity against her. When I saw her struggling against the cold, snow, and ice, and multiple bus routes to get to her place of work each workday morning, I felt sorry for her and frustrated. Brought up to show good manners towards elders, I was annoyed when I gave up a seat to an older person who barely thanked me, only to see that no Canadian was prepared to do the same for my mother. Was it because she looked like a helpless foreigner? There was nothing even superficially Indian about her—not her dress, not her manner of speaking, not even her complexion which was lighter than mine. I had a dark face—darker than hers or my father's—making me feel more like the Prince of Morocco in *The Merchant of Venice*: "Mislike me not for my complexion, / The shadowed livery of the burnished sun, / To whom I am a neighbour, and near bred." Except that I was not as dark as he, nor eager for the burnished sun."

And yet, I did not wish to return to India. When I began specializing in Canadian and Commonwealth Literature at Queen's for my doctorate, I realized that in a radical sense I could never return. Nobody can return to a former self. And there was no nostalgia for what was lost in time because there was always remembrance, which is not quite synonymous with nostalgia. India had never been a paradise for me. My sentimentality was not for the country or my childhood, but for family members who were lost to me because of their own expatriation or because of gaps in genealogical history or because (as with my father's history) they were murdered or eliminated by starvation, thirst, and a broken heart. I arrived in my second country with new expectations, new hopes, new excitement, eager to learn new texts, new angles of vision. What I did not know was the truth that Darwish articulates, that the present does not decide to begin or end. My accent and style of writing had no control over things or my life at the time. I had wanted to modify the perceptions others had of me, but lacking a way of exploring my interior world, I was not really successful. I did not have loyalties to a particular side—neither the Indian, nor the English; neither the Armenian, nor the Canadian. I cannot see myself living in India or Armenia or even England today. I took pride in becoming a Canadian citizen, possessing a Canadian passport, and living within a country that had social guarantees and privileges, and a political, social, and cultural sanity in vivid contrast to the insanities of the United States, most explicitly under Trump. But I don't owe Canada all the pieces of my self.

Perhaps, this was what Darwish means by an "interior solitude." In India, as a teenager, I was in some ways a stranger; and in Canada, in my undergraduate and graduate years, I was an expatriate, a new Canadian with a profound sense of indescribable exile. My family had chosen Canada, but I was not in perfect harmony with it. I suppose I suffered from a psychic deficit. But isn't this one of the ironies of history? As Darwish contends, "history itself is ironic, and it advances without concern for the humanity of its actors or its victims."

To share this view is not to admit despair. It is simply to permit or catalyze meditation. In my senior maturity, I concern myself with the condition of human beings as estranged, wherever they are and however they got to be that way. I recently re-read a poem by Peter Balakian in which he writes of *garod*, that mysterious, almost indefinable feeling that infects many Armenians—and many Jews, Palestinians, or other people who have been displaced or uprooted. And after reflecting on possible meanings, Peter brilliantly crystallizes the feeling in two lines: "Maybe *garod* is about the longing for the native place/between two selves." Or so you think until you come to these lines: "*garod*: the grain chute that spills / into a dark barn which is endless / ... / like the self when it's out of reach." One image building on another, one meaning spilling into another. It's poetry that is both horizontal and vertical.

You refer to Darwish's "inter-immersion," a wanting to live in all cultures. Well, I certainly take pride in my multi-racial background, though to truly live in several cultures would require a multilingualism I have never had, beyond what I consider to be a rudimentary knowledge of French. I have travelled widely, visited many countries, and, so, have had at least a superficial experience with different cultures and ways of life. And I have tried to read poems and non-fiction by writers from most of these countries in order to have a sense of their history and culture. I have tried to listen to their voices. What sharp, sensitive readers may discover in my tetralogy of witness is a conversation of voices. My poems in them (and even the prose in *Pain*) express an internal dialogue between a voice desiring to be present and one manifesting absence of some sort. Perhaps it is only rhetoric expressing different points of view. But, again, to repeat what Darwish contends, I am not alone in place or in time. As a writer, I am my own audience, first and foremost, and as with any audience, truth wears many faces. Several years ago, you referred to my use of a mask in my books, and you used a phrase, "masks of authenticity," which I found particularly apt. To quote from the interview I did with you for Open Book in 2013, "Usually, a mask is a means of disguise or masquerade. It's meant to conceal the identity of the wearer rather than reveal, and the donning of the mask is an act of radical deception. When assuming a persona in writing, the writer is practicing a deception, and we do not need the post-modernists to point this out. But if the mask is adopted, or put in place in order to burrow into another identity, that, perhaps, closely parallels or expresses or explains or explores your own, then the strategy has an authenticity. When I assume Frida Kahlo's voice in *Frida: Paint Me as a Volcano*, it's not to say that I understand women. It's merely to express my empathy with her because we both share an intuitive understanding of human passion in certain situations: love, jealousy, anger, spite, revenge, remorse, ardour, self-violation, et cetera. I am *practicing the art of being private in public*—on behalf of Frida and myself. This is a concept and phrase I borrowed from the late, great William Hutt, who applied it to his own craft. So, yes, when I write about Frida or Derek Jarman or my father or the Armenian genocidal victims or the Armenian artists struggling with the cross-generational, cross-cultural effects of trauma, I'm sharing my preoccupations, stresses, distresses, consolations, et cetera with a reading public—but not simply in a didactic way. I try to be as artful as possible, without sacrificing my core passion." A mask is paradoxical or ironic, but it is also expansive because it permits change or mutation.

To return to *against forgetting*, the poems have antagonistic elements. There is reportage—sights, sounds, smells of Bombay; there is non-poetic fact—as in the poem "The Alimos," prosaic, compressed summary of my mother's siblings; there is etymology in the two opening poems "Forgetting" and "Ways of Forgetting"; there is history (Indian, Anglo-Indian, British colonialism); there is elegy ("Quintets for a Lost Sister"); there is lyricism infused with metaphysical or existential awareness ("The Stars Look Down"); there is summative narrative reflection ("Mimicry"); and there is a major concluding reflection ("Self-Portrait in a New World"). The evident contradictions in form and in myself reflect the contradictions of history, sociology, the huge outer world. My investigation of historical atrocity and denial, colonialism and its aftermaths, cultural displacement, divided identities, and other related issues are the very same concerns of diverse other writers from different cultures and eras, such as Rushdie, Naipaul, Gordimer, Pamuk, Achebe, Walcott, Brodsky, et cetera.

My exilic sense sometimes makes me feel a little like what Reinaldo Arenas portrays as a ghostly shadow in his superbly affecting memoir *Before Night Falls*, his greatest book in my opinion. I am nothing like Arenas in terms of background, sensibility, experience, or literary style. I do not have his "erotic rage," his experiences of brutality, Marxist terrorism, humiliating sexual degradation, ostracism, et cetera. But I do share some of his sense of feeling that there is no place of ultimate rest or equilibrium because as an exile, I live in a world of dreams, sometimes running away from myself. A home is like a beloved's face, and though I call Canada my home, I sometimes feel as if I am deceiving myself. I am at odds with its politics, school system, moneyed elites, literary and theatrical cliques and claques. But I enjoy life in general. I would rather live in Canada than any other place in the world—except in winter, of course. Winter is never my season; snow never my element. So, perhaps the odd existential feeling I have is similar to what was felt by Naipaul, for example—a sense that if one doesn't belong to his "home" and cannot belong fully to anywhere else, then the person is compelled to exist substantially in himself.

What I probably need to do, moving forward as a writer and individual being, is find an equilibrium between my inner self and the outer world I experience in my second country and the places I have travelled or not travelled. The world changes, the world moves on, as every sensitive writer discovers. Even V.S. Naipaul admitted this in a letter he sent me as a response to some questions I had addressed to him while I was writing my dissertation at Queen's in the early seventies. He said, in effect, that he no longer needed to make the pilgrimages he had made earlier to India or the Caribbean or Africa because countries had become more cosmopolitan. Those changes compel writers to change as well in terms of psychic identity and literary experimentation.

EW: I suppose we all retain the "ghostly shadows" Arenas speaks of—parts of us that are built from background, experience, sensibility and concern. As artists and writers, many of us experiment with style, mask, metaphorical appropriation and "alibi"—to use Mahmoud Darwish's term; and we may, at core, all in some way be seeking psychic identity, in its manifoldness. In "rehearsing themes," as you put it in reference to your autobiography-in-progress, you've come, in senior maturity, to concerning yourself with "human beings as estranged, wherever they are and however they got to be that way." Darwish also speaks of estrangement: the stranger as one of the designations of the 'I', "a visitor," yet one to be accepted; "absolutely not negative." This is quite an expansive understanding. In *Palestine As Metaphor*, in the context of "inter-immersion," he tells at length of growing up in Israel, of reading Lorca and Neruda and the Greek tragedies in Hebrew, of his first love—a Jewish woman; one of his best teachers—a Jewish woman; and of his love for the poetry of Yehuda Amichai. He terms Palestine "an alibi"; maintains that "every subject is an alibi"; that the work of the poet is to "create his or her own myths." I wonder if, and to what extent, you find resonance in the ideas of language as homeland, of every subject being an alibi, and of the poet's work being personal and/or collective myth-making.

KG: I have looked up definitions for "alibi," and found these: an excuse; apologia; apology; plea; and pretext. In answer to another of your questions with profound implications, the issues of language as homeland, a subject as alibi, and the poet's work being personal and/or collective myth-making are all intertwined. As Darwish contends, "Language brings the landscape with it." Of course, in his case, it was Hebrew that brought his reading of the Bible and Greek tragedy and subsequent subjects to life. In my case, it was only English, which was my native tongue in a place freed from the colonizer during my early boyhood. The poet in Darwish was not simply Palestinian, but Hebrew as well. In my case, the poet in me has been English, Anglo-Indian, and Armenian (only by English translation). I cannot overlook other international poets, but yet again, only in English translation. Now, what is my alibi for unilingualism (my bilingualism is very limited)? Not learning Hindi or Marathi or Gujarati was a distinct disadvantage to me. I was external or exogenous to Indian custom and philosophy. I was even external to the landscape, in a sense, because I was not seeing it through purely Indian eyes, say, the eyes of a Manohar Malgonkar, or Mulk Raj Anand, or Raja Rao, or R.K. Narayan. My English was a filter through which I viewed India, and I did not seek to fully belong to it. My alibi was my divided heritage, perhaps shaped by England's dishonest alibis for colonialism. The prime European excuse for colonialism was progress—material, industrial, economic, social, political, legislative, cultural. But progress was really for the benefit of Empire. While I did not subscribe to this idea of progress or even accept the excuse, I did share an English prejudice against the old order, the Third World. This attitude, ingested subconsciously, was derived from colonialism, that nefarious doctrine that camouflaged its own barbaric brutalities and intimidation by deliberately degrading whom it sought to colonize. The 'browns, blacks, and yellows' of the world became 'savages', 'niggers,' and 'darkies'. I never subscribed to this colour or racial prejudice, but I probably absorbed a bias against Indian languages, thinking them beneath my dignity or not quite on the same international level as English or of any pragmatic use to me.

Of course, today I am a different person. I no longer see India the way I once did. How could I? I have never returned to India since having left it in 1961. My knowledge of India has widened, of course, but chiefly through Indo-Anglian literature, but my unilingualism remains a form of interior exile. I remain only on the margins of India, cherishing the good things I experienced in the country, relieved at having escaped what I didn't like. But curiously, I have not been fully settled in the landscape of Canada, as I have already outlined earlier. My English is not fully Canadian, nor is my poetry. Because I am continually trying to tell of my own questioning, my own self-examination, I am forging a personal mythology. Yet, because my themes are universal, this mythology is assimilated within a macro-mythology, a collectivity of estrangement.

I write of things that truly exist for me, in my solitary and sometimes rebellious world of contradictions. I have to try and live by the cautionary advice once delivered to Carolyn Forché: "A poet once cautioned me not to live a life that was more vibrant and intense than my inner life, that inner and outer must at least be kept in balance, but if one was to gather strength over the other, let it be the life within." My life has never had quite the intense stress Forché experienced during her adventures in El Salvador; nor has it had the turmoil of Darwish's life. But I am a child of Ararat; that is, someone born to a survivor of genocide. Circumstances decreed that my family and I should find a new homeplace. And I feel a compulsion to articulate a personal mythology which bears witness to my own time and that of my parents.

EW: Again, Keith, you've given a deep and probing response. There are a few threads I'd like to pick up on. You root your unilingualism in a colonial bias you absorbed growing up in India, thinking of Indian languages beneath your dignity, not on the same level as English, and not of any pragmatic use to you. Yet in having made English focal to your métier—writing in the main—in English Canada, you lament your unilingualism, and call it a form of interior exile. I'm wondering if there's a degree to which the "language is damaged"—to borrow George Steiner's term from *Language and Silence*—by the experiences you've had through it, and, in your mature years, by what you've brought to witness in your poetry and memoir work. Though you have not experienced the extremity of what your father endured, or what Carolyn Forché witnessed in El Salvador, your poetic works nonetheless do document extreme experience. They translate the experience of coming through danger, as Forché puts it in her introduction to the 2014 anthology, *Poetry of Witness*, partner volume to her 1993 anthology, *Against Forgetting*. In the introductory Author's Note to your volume of the same name, you write that you used Forché's title because it fits your content in various ways, particularly in the aspects of remembering and *re*/membering. Forché argues for witness as an evidentiary mode rather than a representational mode. She holds that the role of the artist of witness is to testify and that of the reader to witness, to encounter that which happened and share in the experience. What do you make of this distinction?

KG: It's been a long while since I read George Steiner's books, but as much as I hold Steiner in high regard, I do not accept his discourses on language and silence as gospel truths. He was probably right in attacking Noam Chomsky's theory of the same "deep structure" for all languages because I cannot find linguistic universals in all languages. Steiner's argument is predicated on his reading of the Tower of Babel fable: "The bewildering prodigality of tongues had long existed, and had materially complicated the enterprise of men. In trying to build the tower, the nations stumbled on the great secret: that true understanding is possible only when there is silence. They built silently, and there lay the danger to God." I believe otherwise because I see how a plurality of languages and literary creations provoke speech and enrich literature.

A second complication with Steiner's proposition is his own personal biography. As he outlines in *Errata: An Examined Life*, English was one of three languages he used, the others being German and French. Later, a refugee-scholar coached him in Greek and Latin, with Steiner's becoming deeply drawn to Homer, especially *The Iliad.* His background was polyglot, and he eventually taught in *four* languages. So, given this biographical data and the historical evidence of two World Wars, Totalitarianism, and the Shoah, it is possible to see why Steiner thought language can be "damaged." What he says of the inadequacy of language to deal with atrocities of the Holocaust is very similar to the claims of Theodor Adorno, which I have already addressed. I think Steiner is on firmer ground when he argues about the challenges and dangers of translation because of changing conditions of shared exchanges between the original language and the translation. I agree with his strong suggestion that we (especially poets) should pay more careful attention to the "life of language," to the "complex energies of the word in our society and culture." Steiner was also concerned that the Humanities themselves could be damaging if they did not share philosophic and aesthetic experiences which made us more responsive to pain.

It would be up to literary critics to show that my language has been damaged because of my mixed heritage and my inheritance of English as a native language. I am aware that language changes, along with techniques, styles, and tastes. However, I don't concern myself unduly with being up-to-date or writing the way the age demands. I write the way my mind and heart demand. If I were to write according to the critical tastes of the present era, I would feel trapped in a madhouse run by academic theorists or doctrinaire specialist poets: a jargon-bound precarious 'Tower of Babble'. Consider the history of poetics in the 20th century. Ezra Pound demanded a "direct treatment of the 'thing.'" William Carlos Williams insisted on the end of iambic pentameter. Charles Olson propagated the "possibilities of breath." Other poets subscribed to asymmetrical composition, progressive turbulence, poetry as playful "non-sense" (John Ashbery), poetry as algebra (Jorie Graham), poetry as ecstatic incantation (Allen Ginsberg). And then critics to add to the confusion, with Yvor Winters charging that the poem "is not a means to any end, but is in itself an end," only to meet with Kenneth Rexroth's dismissive satire. Critical discourse is one way by which language becomes even more damaged, with critics forcing even greater distance between semantic markers and stable sense.

If, on the other hand, I were to consider Carolyn Forché's idea of language as witness, then I would say that I have felt (not just imagined) some of the pain of my father and his people in the sense of feeling rejected, abused in some way, estranged in some way. My poetry is an attempt to transcend that negative feeling by giving voice to a form of survival and victory—the survival and victory of art. At their best, my poems are, as aftermath, a passing through the experiences of the dead and living, and in some poems the language and structure indicate 'wounding' in line-breaks, imagery, ruptures of utterance, silences and fissures. Perhaps the best examples of what I mean can be found in the poems "A True Portrait of Talaat Pasha," "My Father and I Rarely Touched," "Finishing Sentences," "A Biography of Deracination," and "Fetish of Last Lines"—all from *Poetry Is Blood.* In these poems I hope I create a sense of passing through danger, as was lived by the human subjects of my poetry, and from my own trauma ancestrally passed on to me. So, the poems themselves become not just a retelling or representation but actual experiences in the Latin sense of *ex-piriri*, a crossing through danger, as proposed by Philippe Lacoue-Labarthe in writing about the work of Paul Celan. I show traces of extremity in these poems, my own, the wounds of trauma which, of course, are a bequest or inheritance from my father's trauma. Such poems give evidence against myself but it is not simply politicized or ethical confessionalism. My father as orphaned survivor was a witness; by writing for him, with his spirit and the ghosts of his people in my life, I am also a witness. As Forché phrases it succinctly in "Reading the Living Archives: The Witness of Literary Art," "In the poetry of witness, the poem makes present to us the experience of the other, the poem *is* the experience, rather than a symbolic representation. When we read the poem as witness, we are marked by it and become ourselves witnesses to what it has made present before us. Language incises the page, wounding it with testimonial presence, and the reader is marked by encounter with that presence. Witness begets witness. The text we read becomes a living archive."

Now having reconjured Forché, I realize what you may have meant earlier by questioning whether my language was damaged. And I also wish to pay you a tribute for having recognized from your first reading of *Poetry Is Blood* in manuscript form its versatility and power as poetry of witness. And as you know, Kathryn MacDonald has ranked this book and Goran Simic's *From Sarajevo with Sorrow* among "the best contemporary examples of poetry of witness."

EW: Thank you for yet another detailed and self-searching response, Keith. I have to say that I feel you *do* look here at your work with a critical eye, though you say it would be up to literary critics to show that your language has been damaged by your mixed heritage and inheritance of English as a sole native language. And you *do* allow that you've crossed into danger by way of witnessing your father's experience (in the main), and that you've felt the exile (Is exile a kind of damage?) of unilingualism, which may be a new and distinct extremity in our time. I don't know ... you seem to raise the possibility.

As for standing with Forché's position that the language of witness "wounds with its testimonial presence," this puts both stock in, and onus on, the reader's capacity and willingness to engage and accept that "witness begets witness." George Steiner was less sanguine about the ability of literature and language, whether "damaged" or not, to instill empathy and/or "to enrich and stabilize moral perception." He bemoaned the "thinning" of language as well as the diminishment of reading and engagement of the reader. In *Language and Silence*, he advocates for a re-evaluation of silence—as "in the epistemology of Wittgenstein ... and poetics of Beckett." Interestingly, "silent" and "silence" recur in your "best"-ranked witness collection, *Poetry Is Blood*, in ten of forty poems. Silence is a word that carries deep and nuanced weight in this volume—probably the most multifold of the tetralogy, in terms of stylistic reach. In "A Pilgrimage," "deep silence shrouds my musing, … / from listening to stone," and in the same poem, "Words between us / were silence disguised." Silence is doing at least double-duty here, literally and metaphorically, as is "pilgrimage," though it's titled in the singular. Then there's the "noisy silence" of "Antitheses"; the "long[ing] for silence" of "Komitas"; the "haunting silence" of "Garni Temple." Silence has a crucial speaking role, so to speak. In the profound closing poem, "Fetish of Last Lines," lines and phrases from poems in the collection are gathered to repeat like echoes along history: "how each of us becomes void" and at last "There is only the earth." I would suggest that this collection is also the most searingly un-redemptive.

So, on a more 'active' note—related to remembering and forgetting—this week (October 13, 2020) I attended a Zoom event featuring Israeli author A.B. Yehoshua and his translator Stuart Schoffman, celebrating the publication in English of Yehoshua's new novel *The Tunnel*. In closing, Yehoshua expressed the view that "we have to start to forget too; there is too much remembering now; remembering is becoming dangerous, an obstacle to going forward." He was referring to the Israel-Palestinian conflict. But perhaps he has a broader point. If we are constantly remembering and reminding, we may end up deepening wounds and impeding roads to repair. I realize I'm tilting into the political here, but what is witness if not political? And as we are living in quite singular 'crisis time', in which Armenia, too, is again embroiled in active conflict with Azerbaijan over land and rule, with Turkey and Russia on the 'sidelines', I'm wondering if you are feeling a heightened or renewed sense of witness relationship. How do you feel about A.B. Yehoshua's view vis-à-vis too much remembering? Is there a sense in which remembering and forgetting need to be brought into balance at this time, in order to go forward? If so, how as writers, can we contribute?

KG: I think all writers, especially poets, wish that they could have close, careful readings of their work, and I shall always be grateful to you for what you have so wonderfully discovered and revealed to me. I was not aware of the frequency of the words silence or silent in those poems because, of course, I was writing them separately and not necessarily in the sequence in which they occur in the printed book. Like all good critics, you have gone deep into the text, and sought connections, links, patterns. Such careful reading honours my poems, acknowledges that they are more than documentary pictorials of historical atrocity. You are certainly correct in reading *Poetry Is Blood* as a "searingly un-redemptive" work. Indeed, I am struck now at the difference in tone between *Children of Ararat* (especially the optimistic tone of the Afterword) and *PIB*. But once more, a poet's life and outlook changes in time because of experiences. I still consider myself an optimistic person, at least in the sense of believing that the human race can survive catastrophes (both manmade and created by nature), though much depends on the actuality of human rationality and goodness. Survival is at the heart of remembering, for remembering is a 'memory museum' (to steal Susan Sontag's term from *Regarding the Pain of Others*). What we first remember in such a museum is destruction (suffering, slaughter, genocide), but photographic and textual evidence are more than reminders of death, failure, or victimization. They are crucial for invoking the miracle of survival.

I agree with Sontag that to aim at the perpetuation of memories means, inevitably, that one has undertaken the task of continually renewing, of creating memories, whether this is aided by "the impress of iconic photograph" or not. Well, my poems about the Armenian genocide can often be read as photographs or moments of narrative about lives lived, lost, and reconfigured. The beautiful thing about poetry of witness is that it is not just a collection of mental photographs where only the photographs are remembered. Referring to literal photographs, Sontag asks what is the point of exhibiting such photographs? "To awaken indignation? To make us feel 'bad'; that is, to appall and sadden? To help us mourn?" She knows they are beyond punishment. But sympathy in itself, the "imaginary proximity to the suffering inflicted on others" is not enough to justify the images. On one hand, as Sontag asserts, "Our sympathy proclaims our innocence as well as our impotence." On the other hand, sympathy also shows that our feelings are not dulled; only passivity or torpor dulls feeling. So, what is the active essence in sympathy or remembering? I think it is the reflection, the meditation in poetry. To write good poetry of witness, the poet needs to balance critical cynicism or realism about the world with an aching relationship with the dead. The poet turns his own images into more than mere *memento mori.* Of course, the weight of this action or burden is immense—even traumatic. And, perhaps, the action is frustratingly Sisyphean. But conscience rebukes the weak, the complacent, the pessimistic. And to suffer from bad or guilty conscience is death-in-life.

So, keeping in mind what A.B. Yehoshua says about the danger of too much remembrance, how do I go forward at yet another perilous time for Armenians and the world in general? By writing poems *against forgetting the essentials of human value* by creating poems that crystallize *the power and capaciousness of imagination*, poems that celebrate the gift for *reconfiguring reality as art.* It is for our art that we will be remembered, not forgotten. Writing well is, indeed, good (though not necessarily the best) revenge against perpetrators of atrocity, mendacity, ethnic and cultural genocide.

EW: I'm heartened by this response, Keith, particularly by your salute to imagination in poetry as a force for remembering—against forgetting—the essentials of "*human value*." Turkish Nobel laureate Orhan Pamuk has also affirmed—most explicitly in his essay collection *Other Colors,* —the importance of imagination, through literature, for awakening sensibilities, and for expanding awareness of cultural- and identity-diversity; the experience of the other. Pamuk has been criminalized by his government for his activism in imagining/witnessing—in his fiction and as a Turkish citizen—the Armenian genocide during WW1 and the more recent suppression of the Kurdish minority in Turkey. Imagination in both life and art, it would seem, comes with a cost, and yet is essential to empathy, to the humanizing, ethical 'I-Thou' relationship; to standing in the place of the other and recognizing that each of us is both self and other. I want to side with you in holding that "writing well is good revenge against mendacity and atrocity," and that "it is for our art that we will be remembered." With you, I want to be optimistic about the possibility of "reconfiguring reality through art." There's so much reconfiguring work to do in our time.

And on this note, I'd like to turn to your recently published collection, *Mini Musings: Miniature Thoughts on Theatre and Poetry*. This witty and scintillating collection, modelled on American playwright Sarah Ruhl's collection, *100 Essays I Don't Have Time to Write*, contains not quite 100 short "vignettes, anecdotes, and impressionistic perspectives" on two of your life-loves—theatre and poetry—as well as pieces on other "curiosities and obsessions." I would say that these pieces are entertainments, as they *are* entertaining, except that that would take away from their fine-mindedness and sincere engagement. I'm thinking of your strong bid for "a role for a literary audience ... as an active respondent to questions, suggestions, and lines of argument." Unlike new Nobel laureate, American poet Louise Glück, whose epigraph to Ruhl's collection you quote in your Preface, you state that you seek not so much to "finish [your] own sentences" (as has been avowedly important to Glück), but rather to provoke further contemplation or meditation. You make no apology for your provocativeness or cosmopolitanism. These pieces are not meant to be 'famous last words', so to speak, but rather "opening gambits." You attribute this preference for 'unfinishedness' to one of your favourite Canadians and literary subjects, the late great Shakespearean actor William Hutt, who, you relate, left you pondering the implications of the "unfinished." I might add that one of my favourite writers and literary subjects, Franz Kafka, was also famous for leaving work deliberately unfinished—perhaps one of the reasons his work has continued to be revisited, reread, and remains inexhaustibly ponderable. So, I'm wondering if you yourself have something to add to your unfinished musing—in the context of some of your other subjects in the collection: the private and the public self; identities and the "need to be noticed"; "one's real life and the life one does not lead"; masking and coding versus responsibility in poetry (Is there a versus?); and the very topical topic of "cultural appropriation."

KG: My subtitle for the collection is "Miniature Thoughts on Theatre and Poetry," and like all my book titles, a certain amount of thought has gone into how I settle on a title. You have accurately represented my driving motivations: the essays are not "famous" or "final" last words; they are "opening gambits," which implies that they are open to further reflection, new or contrary perspectives. I don't pretend that they are "inexhaustibly ponderable," because they are springboards rather than finished arguments. In fact, many—if not most—of them are simply small windows opening to very large fields. But isn't this image particularly apt for a poet? Great artists, great playwrights, great poets have much wider, larger windows than mediocre ones, and their fields of vision are also wider, larger. These writers revel in ambiguities, which means uncertainties, possible connotations—but not formlessness. The best writers are not dogmatic philosophers or theologians, doctrinaire politicians, desiccated educators, or dyed-in-the-wool bureaucrats who are helplessly in love with tight categories, self-assured mission statements or tedious guidebooks. I am no evangelist, either in theatre or poetry. When it comes to Theatre, I know that there is no single way of staging Shakespeare or a definitive, full-proof method for acting. When it comes to Poetry, there is no formula for extraordinary poetry. There is no single way or path to any truth because each man's truth is his own, though the deepest truth always shows a connection to the real world outside himself.

I criticize contemporary Canadian playwrights and directors for their narrow visions and inferior modes of representation. Too many Canadian plays are stuck in sheer documentary mode, and what they tell me is less than what I can discover in a worthy newspaper or magazine, though worthy ones are getting harder to find today. Or they attempt to "shock" without any art informing their tactics or any deep content justifying the "shock." On the other hand, Canadian poetry has a much wider, larger field of practitioners, and a much higher level of achievement, though even here, I find that few of my contemporaries address the huge realities of a very turbulent, very disturbing world.

Shakespeare has always been my greatest model in literature and in poetry, not simply because of his power, depth, and virtuosity of expression. He cripples all criticism of his being culturally inappropriate because he created (what Trevor Nunn calls) "a theatre of recognition, a theatre wherein we see ourselves, we see human behaviour as we encounter it, as we feel the need to understand it. We can be shamed by him because of that recognition, or we can be elevated by him because of that recognition."

It is from Shakespeare that I most derive my use of personae in poetry, from my beginner's collection (*Reservoir of Ancestors*), to *Frida, Blue, Georgia and Alfred*, and parts of *Children of Ararat* and *Poetry Is Blood*. We have already discussed the implications of masks and codes, but I need to add that using personae is another way of seeking attention the way an actor would when playing a role. It is also a way of leading a real life parallel to the life one does not really live. The poets I most admire or whom I am most passionate about are those who make me recognize my fellow-man and the world that circumscribes me and fellow-man. This explains my frequent mixture of lyric, anti-lyric, monologue, list poem, ekphrasis, collage, cento, et cetera, as well as my enthusiasm for the best Canadian First Nations poets (gay, lesbian, transgender), the great Palestinian/Arab and Israeli poets, the wonderfully potent new black American poets, and the very accomplished CanAsian or BritAsian poets who address issues of trauma, identity, cultural survival, and such. However, I do not read poetry with a score-sheet near me. I don't check off boxes. I don't create in order to deliver a message. The words themselves, and the design they create are the message. Poetry, like Theatre, is a sensory experience, and the best of it for me is visceral—but channelled through craft that *could* extend their after-life, which is to say their potential to endure in a reader's memory. You notice that I say "could" rather than "will" because the verdict of posterity is unpredictable. Taste changes, as do fashions or modes of writing. But what lasts is the passion *of* or *in* a piece. Of course, I admire poets with exquisite, flawless technique, but I feel flushes of greater and deeper excitement when I read certain poems of Shakespeare, Whitman, Rimbaud, Thomas, Plath, Layton, Walcott, Darwish, Celan, et cetera. I also thrill to poems by Ocean Vuong, Jericho Brown, Rigoberto Gonzalez, and all who show me the faces of man in all their hideousness, ecstasies, and pain, and do so with powerful skill.

Speaking of my own unfinished or future work, I want to be read, heard, understood, intelligently interpreted—all very ordinary expectations of a writer. My greatest responsibility is to myself or the truth of myself and an accurate representation of the worlds that made me. Another responsibility, and a very large one, is to the craft of writing. Chaucer correctly maintained, "the lyf so short, the craft so long to lerne." Let my readers decide on where I have succeeded or failed—but only after they have read me carefully.

Bibliography

Nonfiction

Hugh Hood. Boston: Twayne, 1983.

Hugh Hood and His Works. Toronto: ECW Press, 1985.

William Hutt: A Theatre Portrait. Oakville: Mosaic Press, 1988.

Leon Rooke and His Works. Toronto: ECW Press, 1989.

A Well-Bred Muse: Selected Theatre Writings 1978–1988. Oakville: Mosaic Press, 1991.

George Bernard Shaw and Christopher Newton: Explorations of Shavian Theatre. Oakville: Mosaic Press, 1993.

The Making of 'My Fair Lady'. Toronto: ECW Press, 1993. Second printing, 1998. Third printing, 2004. Rights sold to Firefly Book Club, Doubleday Book Club, Reynolds & Hearn.

The Making of 'Gypsy'. Toronto: ECW Press, 1994. Second printing, 1998. Third printing, 2004. Rights sold to Firefly Book Club, Doubleday Book Club, Reynolds & Hearn.

The Making of 'West Side Story'. Toronto: ECW Press, 1995. Second printing, 1998. Third printing, 2004. Rights sold to Firefly Book Club, Doubleday Book Club, Reynolds & Hearn.

The Making of 'Cabaret'. Oakville: Mosaic Press, 1999. Second printing, 2004. Rights sold to Firefly Book Club, Doubleday Book Club, Reynolds & Hearn.

Pain: Journeys Around My Parents. Oakville: Mosaic Press, 2000.

The Making of 'Guys and Dolls'. Oakville: Mosaic Press, 2002. Second printing, 2004. Rights sold to Firefly Book Club, Doubleday Book Club, Reynolds & Hearn.

The Making of 'Cabaret' (New Revised Edition), New York: Oxford University Press, 2011.

Accidental Genius: The Pantheon of Modern American Poets. Toronto: Guernica Editions, 2015.

Lerner and Loewe's 'My Fair Lady'. London: Routledge, 2016.

William Hutt: Soldier Actor. Toronto: Guernica Editions, 2017.

Colours to the Chameleon: Canadian Actors on Shakespeare. Toronto: Guernica Editions, 2019.

Mini-Musings: Miniature Essays on Theatre and Poetry. Toronto: Guernica Editions, 2020.

Pieces of My Self. Toronto: Guernica Editions, 2023.

Poetry

Reservoir of Ancestors. Oakville: Mosaic Press, 2003.

Frida: Paint Me As a Volcano / Frida: Un Volcan de Souffrance. Ottawa: Buschek Books, 2004.

Blue: The Derek Jarman Poems. Winnipeg: Signature Editions, 2008.

Children of Ararat. Calgary: Frontenac House, 2010.

Moon on Wild Grasses. Toronto: Guernica Editions, 2013.

Georgia and Alfred. Toronto: Quattro Books, 2015.

Poetry Is Blood. Toronto: Guernica Editions, 2018.

Against Forgetting. Calgary: Frontenac House, 2019.

in the bowl of my eye. Toronto: Mawenzi House, 2022.

Finger to Finger. Calgary: Frontenac House, 2022.

Three-Way Renegade: $amuel $teward Without Apology. Calgary: Frontenac House, 2024.

Poetry Chapbooks

Samson's Hair and Other Satiric Fantasies. Toronto: Micro Prose, 2004.

SCAN Cancer Poems. (Disability Series: Number Twenty-Two). Victoria: Frog Hollow Press, 2021.

Areté. Toronto: The Ontario Poetry Society, 2024.

Elegy for Maria. New Liskeard, ON: A&B Digital Printing, 2024.

As Editor

William Hutt: Masks and Faces. Oakville: Mosaic Press, 1995.

Tiananmen Flight by Patrick S. Nicholson. Oakville: Mosaic Press, 2001.

In The Museum of Leonardo Da Vinci by Jeffrey Round. Toronto: Tightrope Books, 2014.

Side Effects: a footloose journey to the apocalypse by S. Montana Katz. Toronto: Guernica Editions, 2020.

As Contributor

This Is My Best: Poems Selected by Ninety-one Poets. Toronto: Coach House Press, 1976. ("Voss in the Desert").

Tributaries: An Anthology: Writer to Writer. Barry Dempster, ed. Oakville, ON: Mosaic Press/Valley Editions, 1978. ("Armenian Elegy").

Aurora: New Canadian Writing 1978. Morris Wolfe, ed. Toronto: Doubleday Canada Ltd., 1978. ("Adam Meeting Eve"; "sleeping with th grass"; "ths lust ium in luv with").

The Question as Commitment: A Symposium. Montreal: Thomas More Institute Papers/77. Montreal: Perry Printing, 1979.

Contemporary Criticism, Vol. 9. Michigan: Gale Research, 1978. ("The Desert and the Garden: The Theme of Completeness in *Voss*").

None Genuine Without This Signature by Hugh Hood. Downsview, ON; ECW Press, 1980. ("Introduction")

Spotlight on Drama (A teaching and resource guide to Canadian plays. Constance Brissenden, ed. Toronto: The Writers' Development Trust, 1981. ("The Family: Introduction").

The Oxford Companion to Canadian Literature, William Toye, ed. Toronto: Oxford University Press, 1983. ("Buell, John"; "Gutteridge, Don").

The Montreal Storytellers, J.R. (Tim) Struthers, ed. Montreal: Véhicule Press, 1985. ("In The End, A Beginning: The Montreal Storytellers").

Beacham's Popular Fiction in America. Walton Beacham, ed. Washington, D.C.: Beacham Publishing, 1986 and 1987. ("John Buell"; "Guy Vanderhaeghe; "Timothy Findley"; "Alice Munro").

Dictionary of Literary Biography: Canadian Writers Since 1960. W.H. New, ed. Detroit, Michigan: Gale, 1986. (*Bertram Warr*)

Magill's Masterplots II. (World Fiction Series). California: Salem Press, 1988. ("Heinrich Boll," "Josef Skvorecky," "Jun'ichiro Tanizaki").

Great Lives from History. California: Salem Press, 1988. ("Galen").

The Oxford Companion to Canadian Theatre. Eugene Benson and L.W. Conolly, eds. Toronto, Oxford, New York: Oxford University Press, 1989. ("John Pennoyer"; "Michael Eagan"; "Les Canadiens"; Rick Salutin").

Masterplots: Juvenile and Young Adult Fiction. California: Salem Press, 1990. ("Tom Brown's School Days").

Magill's Great Events from History II. Michigan: Salem Press, 1993. ("Olivier's National Theatre"; "Nijinsky Dances *Afternoon of a Faun*"; "Fokine Stages *Les Sylphides*").

On-Stage and Off-Stage: English Canadian Drama in Discourse. Albert-Reiner Glaap and Rolf Althof, eds. St. John's, NF: Breakwater Books, 1996. ("Henry Beissel: Tragicomic Moralist").

Magill's Encyclopedia of Propaganda. California: Salem Press, 1997. ("John Buchan").

The Sixties in America. California: Salem Press, 1997. ("The French Connection").

Encyclopedia of Family Life. California: Salem Press, 1998. ("Male Circumcision," "Jerome Bruner,'" "Arnold Gesell", "Strawberry Hemangioma" and "Warts").

The Sixties in America. California: Salem Press, 1998. ("Jane Fonda" and "John Cheever").

Magill's Medical Guide: Pediatrics. California: Salem Press, 1998. ("Masturbation," "Hymen," "Testicular Torsion," and "Frostbite").

Encyclopedia of Civil Rights in America. California: Salem Press, 1998. ("The Long Walk Home").

Biographical Encyclopedia of the Twentieth Century. California: Salem Press, 1999. ("Mahatma Gandhi," "W.A.C. Bennett," "Vincent Massey," "Robert Borden," "Jeanne Sauve," and "Joey Smallwood").

Racial and Ethnic Relations in America. California: Salem Press, 1999. ("Vietnamese Canadians," "Refugees: Canadian Policy," "African Canadians," "Arab Canadians," "Racial and Ethnic Jokes and Humor").

Encyclopedia of World Geography. California: Salem Press, 2000. ("Gazetteer of Southeast Asia').

Encyclopedia of Literary Places. California: Salem Press, 2002. ("*Henry IV*," "*Measure for Measure*," "*The Merchant of Venice*," "*Patience*," "*Private Lives*," "Tevye," "*Twelfth Night*," "*Who's Afraid of Virginia Woolf*").

Contributors

Born in Cairo, Egypt, ATOM EGOYAN is an Academy Award nominated Canadian writer and director who has created a body of work for film, stage, and television. Emerging in the 1980s as part of the Toronto New Wave, he made his career breakthrough with *Exotica*, a film set in a strip club. Egoyan's most critically acclaimed film is the drama *The Sweet Hereafter*, for which he received two Academy Award nominations. His art installations have also been exhibited around the world, including the Venice Biennale and the Tate Modern. Egoyan has won many international prizes, including five awards at the Cannes Film Festival. He has won the Governor General Award for Performing Arts, and is a Companion of the Order of Canada.

BRIAN BARTLETT has published fifteen collections and chapbooks of poetry, three prose books of nature writing, and a gathering of prose on poetry. He has also edited selected volumes by Don Domanski, Dorothy Roberts and James Reaney, a compilation of essays about Don McKay, and Alden Nowlan's *Collected Poems*. Bartlett's poetry collection, *The Astonishing Room* (Frontenac House, 2024), was shortlisted for the 2025 Al and Eurithe Purdy Poetry Prize. Bartlett has lived in Kjipuktuk/Halifax since 1990. During the late 1970s and early 1980s, he often reviewed books for the Montreal *Gazette*, as did Keith Garebian.

DAVID BATEMAN is a novelist, arts journalist, and performance poet whose work has been presented internationally. He has taught creative writing at various post-secondary institutions across the country. His four collections of poetry were published by Frontenac House from 2005 to 2014. His collaborative long poem with Hiromi Goto, *Wait Until Late Afternoon*, was shortlisted for the Relit Award in 2010, and his first collection, *Invisible Foreground*, was nominated for the Stephan G. Stephansson Award in 2006. His first novel, *DR SAD*, published by University of Calgary Press in 2020, was a finalist in the LGBTQ+ INDIE Awards. *A Mad Bent Diva*, a collection of short stories and creative nonfiction, was published by Hidden Brook Press in 2017.

ROBIN BREON (1948-2023) was an independent arts journalist with a publishing history spanning many years. He held an undergraduate degree in theatre and communications and a master's degree in education. His reviews, articles and cultural essays have appeared in a wide range of media, including the popular press as well as academic journals. He was a founding member of the Toronto Drama Bench (1972) and served on the executive board of the Canadian Theatre Critics' Association, the successor organization to the TDB. As a playwright, he authored *The African Roscius (Being the Life and Times of Ira Aldridge)*, produced by Black Theatre Canada at the Alumnae.

The 4th Poet Laureate of Toronto (2012-15) and the 7th Parliamentary/Canadian Poet Laureate (2016-17), GEORGE ELLIOTT CLARKE is a celebrated artist in song, drama, fiction, screenplay, essays, and poetry. Born in Windsor, Nova Scotia, in 1960, George was educated at the University of Waterloo, Dalhousie University, and Queen's University. He is also a pioneering scholar of African-Canadian literature. A professor of English at the University of Toronto, George has taught at Duke, McGill, the University of British Columbia, and Harvard. He holds eight honorary doctorates, plus appointments to the Order of Nova

Scotia and the Order of Canada at the rank of Officer. His recognitions include the Pierre Elliott Trudeau Fellows Prize, the Governor-General's Award for Poetry, the National Magazine Gold Award for Poetry, the Dartmouth Book Award for Fiction, the Eric Hoffer Book Award for Poetry (US), and the Dr. Martin Luther King Jr. Achievement Award.

Montreal-born JOAN HENEY was a professional actress on radio, stage, and film for over fifty years. As Joan Watts (her maiden name), she had the distinction of having been an apprentice at the inaugural Stratford Festival, Ontario, 1953, and appearing in productions directed by Tyrone Guthrie and Michael Langham. Her largest stage credits include feature and lead roles at the Lennoxville Festival, the Saidye Bronfman Theatre, Nightwood, Buddies in Bad Times, Lovers and Madmen Theatre, and at theatres in Orillia and Barrie. She was nominated for a Dora Award for Outstanding Performance in a Principal Role in 1996 for her performance in Ned Vucovic's, *The Misfit*. She is also the author of *Road Dances* (Landsdowne Press, 1984), a poetry collection.

LAURENCE HUTCHMAN grew up in Toronto. He received his PhD from the Université de Montreal and has taught at several universities. For twenty-three years, he was a professor of English literature at the Université de Moncton at the Edmundston Campus. Hutchman has published thirteen books of poetry, coedited the anthology *Coastlines: The Poetry of Atlantic Canada*, and edited two volumes of *In the Writers' Words*. His poetry has received many grants and awards, including the Alden Nowlan Award for Excellence, and has been translated into numerous languages. In 2017, he was named poet laureate of Emery, north Toronto.

KEVIN IRIE is a Japanese-Canadian poet. His poems have been published in Canada, the States, Australia, and England, have been broadcast on CBC Radio and have been translated into Spanish, French, and Japanese. He has twice been long-listed for the CBC Poetry Prize. His book *The Colour of Eden* was a finalist for the 1997 Toronto Book Award. *Angel Blood: The Tess Poems,* was nominated for the 2005 ReLit Award. His book, *Viewing Tom Thomson: A Minority Report* was a finalist for the 2013 Acorn-Plantos People's Poetry Award and the Toronto Book Award. His most recent, *The Tantramar Re-Vision* (McGill-Queen's University Press, 2021) was picked by the CBC as one of the Spring Poetry Books 2021 and by *Quill & Quire Magazine* as part of their 2021 Summer Reading Guide. He lives in Toronto.

MICHELINE MAYLOR attained a Ph.D. at the University of Newcastle Upon Tyne in English Language and Literature with a specialization in Creative Writing and 20th Century Canadian Poetics. She is retired from teaching Creative Writing at Mount Royal University in Calgary, where she won the 2015 Teaching Excellence Award, and the 2018 Distinguished Faculty Award. She is also a Poet Laureate Emerita of Calgary (2016-18) and was awarded the Queen's Platinum Jubilee Award for literary contributions to Alberta in 2022. Her most recent book, *The Bad Wife* (University of Alberta Press, 2021), won the BPAA Robert Kroetsch Award for best book of Alberta poetry.

JIM NASON, a freelance teacher, artist, and writer, is the author of eight volumes of poetry, a short story collection, and three novels. He has been a finalist for the CBC Literary Award in both the fiction and poetry categories. His poetry book *Rooster, Dog, Crow* was shortlisted for the 2019 Raymond Souster Award, and his poems have been included in anthologies across the

United States and Canada, including *Best Canadian Poetry* in 2008, 2010, and 2014. For over two decades, Jim has facilitated numerous writing workshops and/or participated as an author or instructor at literary venues such as the Edinburgh Fringe Festival, the Toronto International Festival of Authors, and the Winnipeg International Writers Festival.

JOHN OUGHTON hails from Guelph, Ontario, has lived in Iraq, Egypt, and Japan, and now resides in Toronto's Beaches area. He studied at York University with Irving Layton, Eli Mandel, Frank Davey, and Miriam Waddington, and completed summer sessions at Naropa University's Jack Kerouac School of Disembodied Poetics in Boulder, Colorado, where he was research assistant to Allen Ginsberg and Anne Waldman. He has published close to 500 articles, reviews, blogs, and interviews, and six poetry collections, most recently, *The Universe and All That* (Ekstasis Editions, 2023). He has also published a mystery novel, *Death by Triangulation* (NeoPoiesis Press, 2015), and *Higher Teaching: A Handbook for New Postsecondary Faculty* (Guernica Editions, 2021). John is a retired Professor of Learning and Teaching at Centennial College, Toronto.

FELICE PICANO's stories, novels and nonfiction are translated into seventeen languages, and include national and international bestsellers. Four of his plays have been produced. He received awards for poetry, drama, short stories, novels and memoirs. His duology, *Pursuit: A Victorian Entertainment* and *Pursued: Lillian's Story* were published in 2021 and 2022 respectively; Volumes 2 and 3 of his Sci-Fi *City on a Star* Trilogy, *The Betrothal at Usk* and *A Bard on Hercular*, were also published in 2021 and 2022. In 2024, ReQueered Tales reprinted Picano's earliest novels and Beautiful Dreamer Press presented his banned book, *Ambidextrous: The Secret Lives of Children.*

Picano lectured on Vintage Hollywood and screenwriting and lived in West Hollywood. He passed away in Los Angeles on March 12, 2025.

JEFFREY ROUND is an award-winning author, playwright, and filmmaker. His books include the seven-volume Lambda-winning Dan Sharp mysteries, the Bradford Fairfax comic mysteries, the ReLit-nominated poetry collection *In the Museum of Leonardo da Vinci* (edited by Keith Garebian), and the acclaimed war novel, *The Honey Locust.* He directed Agatha Christie's stage classic, *The Mousetrap*, for three of its 27 record-breaking years at Toronto Truck Theatre. His 2022 music video, *Gone Again*, won the Luis Buñuel Memorial Award. His latest book, *The Sulphur Springs Cure,* a historical whodunit from Cormorant Books, was called "an extremely satisfying reading experience" by the *Toronto Star*.

DAVID and ROSE SCOLLARD founded Frontenac House, a book publisher specializing in Canadian poetry, in 1999. Between that date and 2015, when they retired from the business, they published approximately 115 books, mostly poetry, although Frontenac also brought out books on art, aviation, and other subjects. Prior to Frontenac House, David spent most of his career working with other book publishers such as Ryerson Press, McClelland and Stewart, and McClelland and Stewart West; he also worked several years in the commercial sector in Calgary. Previously, Rose was cofounder, with Alexandria Patience and Nancy Jo Cullen, of Maenad Productions, Western Canada's first woman-centered theatre group. Her play *Shea of the White Hands*, a modern-day version of Tristan and Isolde, was a finalist for the Susan Smith Blackburn Prize; her anthology of radio plays, *Love and War Western Style*, will be published by the University of Calgary Press in 2025.

DOROTHY SJÖHOLM is a poet and short story writer who lives in Barrie, Ontario with her husband John, and a bossy pup named Maxwell. Her work has appeared in print and online journals in Canada, England, and USA, and has won awards from various Arts Councils and writers' communities in Ontario. After self-publishing *Holding the Mirror* and "wait for the final explosion," she completed an MFA in Creative Writing through the University of British Columbia in 2015, and in 2019 Piquant Press published her novella in verse, *why the telephone stopped ringing*, a subsequent version of her MFA thesis.

TESSA PAUCHA was a student of Keith Garebian in 1969-1970. She walked several different career paths after that, all of them related to writing and language, though only peripherally to her first love: literature. Now happily retired from earning a living, Tessa is delighting in exploring her own voice at her home in Toronto.

Born in Jerusalem, JIRAIR TUTUNJIAN immigrated to Canada soon after graduating from high school in 1964. He graduated with a B.A. in journalism from Ryerson in late 1968, and in 1970 became the youngest editor of a large-circulation magazine, subsequently managing and editing six award-winning consumer and business magazines till 2008 when he became editor of the web publication keghart.org. His journalism has allowed him to travel to more than 90 countries. He has written close to a thousand articles, four books, and serves as nonfiction editor of *Exile Quarterly*. His latest book, independently published, is *Armenian Greats—Known and Unknown.*

ELANA WOLFF is the author of eight collections of poems, a collection of essays on poems, and original translations from the Hebrew, with Menachem Wolff, of poems by Georg

Mordechai Langer. Elana's writing is widely published in Canada and internationally, has been translated into French, Spanish, Chinese and Persian, and has garnered numerous awards, including the F.G. Bressani Prize and the Canadian Jewish Literary Award for Poetry. She has taught English for Academic Purposes at York University in Toronto and at The Hebrew University in Jerusalem. She currently lives and works in Thornhill, Ontario—the ancestral land of the Haudenosaunee and Huron-Wendat First Nations. Elana's cross-genre Kafka-quest work, *Faithfully Seeking Franz*, received the 2024 Canadian Jewish Literary Award in the category of Jewish Thought and Culture.

Printed by Imprimerie Gauvin
Gatineau, Québec